DAVY CROCKETT

GREAT BRANCHES STRUCK THE TAVERN

DAVY CROCKETT

by

CONSTANCE ROURKE

Illustrated by
JAMES MAC DONALD

HARCOURT, BRACE AND COMPANY
NEW YORK

B
Crockett
c. 8

For my great aunts

Minerva and Elizabeth Mayfield

who knew stories

about Davy Crockett

FOREWORD

When a country is young it discovers its heroes, and these are not always leaders in battle. They may only be men who have had adventures others long for. They may show admired traits, or strange ones. They may talk or laugh in a fashion which others enjoy. Always stories are told about them.

Davy Crockett was one of these. Springing from adventurous stock, he was born soon after the Revolution in the river country of Tennessee, not far from the Blue Ridge, when the Cherokees were still powerful and the Creeks still on the warpath. He knew wild life as few have known it, and he became the most noted hunter of his time. Even while he was an obscure backwoodsman comical tales and high talk could be heard about him, and his own humor had fame among the people of his region. When he emerged from the wilderness and appeared in the East as Congressman, he suddenly seemed to the popular imagination all that had been known or guessed about life in the western woods or on the western waters. There was truth in this: even in the most soaring of the many tall tales about Crockett there was truth. Fantastic as these were, they belonged to the western country—its great rivers, trees, high winds, storms, earthquakes, wild beasts.

FOREWORD

About no single American figure have so many legends clustered. After Crockett's death whole cycles of legendary tales were told about him that form a rich outflowering of the American imagination. But side by side with the legend is the living figure. The core of fact in Crockett's life is plain. Documents and letters are available, with records of his talk, his decisions, his principles, all set down freely in his own time and afterward. Closely knit with these are the decisions and the talk of his contemporaries. At a few points, where direct evidence is lacking, its place is taken by traditions interwoven to form solid strands, linking events.

The full substance of Crockett's career has never been revealed. He has been pictured as uncouth and illiterate, but there is abundant testimony to prove that he was neither. In a direct and simple fashion he was engaged in conflicts which now seem to us of prime importance because their outcome has had a determining effect in the life of the nation. But this phase of his career has been largely forgotten. Crockett's "Narrative" and the other books ascribed to him reveal only portions of his life. A full biography has seemed his due, in which his purposes, his rash and engaging character, the circumstances of his many adventures, and the bold legends about him should all have a place.

CONTENTS

ILLUSTRATIONS

DAVY CROCKETT

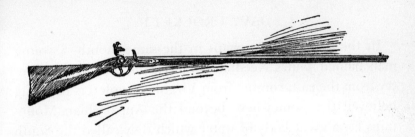

1

CRADLED IN A SNAPPING
TURTLE'S SHELL

IN THE early summer of 1673 a small party of white men floated in two canoes down the wide waters of the Mississippi. They had passed the mouth of the Ohio, and soon discovered rising bluffs on the eastern shore of the great river. Presently Indians were seen among the trees, armed and observant. They belonged to a small tribe ruled by the powerful Chickasaws. The travelers spoke to them in the Huron language, which this tribe did not understand, and held aloft a feathered calumet given them by the Illinois Indians to the north for use as a friendly sign on their journey. The white men landed, were welcomed, and joined the tribe in a feast of buffalo meat, bear's oil, and delicious white plums.

The travelers were Father Marquette and Sieur Jolliet, and the country they briefly visited along its western boundary was later to be known as Tennessee.

In the same year, perhaps in the same month, a young man named James Needham entered the Tennessee country from the east, coming from Virginia. Explorers had long believed that somewhere beyond the Appalachian Mountains lay a great body of water which they called the South Sea. With eight Indians and a white servant Needham crossed the mountains, following ancient buffalo paths and trails, and at last from an escarpment of the Blue Ridge he saw, not a great sea, but wide rolling valleys where clear waters coursed down the green lower hills like long sprays of silvery fern.

Descending, Needham crossed many small streams and paused at a Cherokee village, where his party was hospitably received. He was probably the first white man to enter the Tennessee country from the east. On a second journey into this region he was killed by an Indian servant, and it was many years before other white men ventured there again.

For almost another century this rich land remained in the possession of the Indians. On the east, in the valleys bordering Virginia and the Carolinas, were the Cherokees. To the south, in the broad territory that was to become Georgia and Alabama and Mississippi, the Creeks held sway. To the west, where Father Marquette had landed, the Chickasaws still flourished. To the north was that dark and bloody ground called Kentucky, where no Indians dwelt but where many came for hunting.

Slowly white men made their way from the eastern colonies into the Tennessee country, as fur traders and trappers, and for the land—to seize great tracts of it but not to dwell there. Then the American Revolution began. The battle of King's Mountain was fought, and before the Revolution was ended a few settlers had come over the Blue Ridge from the Carolinas and Virginia to build cabins.

Among these was a David Crockett, of sound stock and Irish descent, with his wife and grown sons and daughters, some of them married with children of their own. Either Crockett or his son John—perhaps both—had fought at the battle of King's Mountain. With this David Crockett's gear was "a parsel of books," weighing fifteen pounds. The family settled in the valley of the Nolachucky, not far from the mountains they had crossed, on land from which the Cherokees had receded.

A roving band of Creeks or Cherokees descended swiftly one day and killed the older Crockett, his wife, and some of his children, wounded one son, left him for dead, and carried off another. John Crockett and his family were living only a few miles distant, at the mouth of the Limestone where it pours into the Nolachucky, but the Indians did not attack his cabin. A short time after the raid, on the 17th of August, 1786, a son was born in this cabin to John and Rebecca Crockett, their ninth child. He was named for his grandfather, David, and he became the famous Davy Crockett of American history and legend.

John Crockett was unlucky. He built a mill on a small creek to grind corn for his distant neighbors, and in a stormy April the mill was carried away by high water. He moved to a point on the Holston near a ford where a trail from the Blue Ridge crossed the river and wound away through the forest. This was to become the road from Abingdon to Knoxville. Here he established a small tavern, a humble affair of logs with a few rudely partitioned rooms.

The country was still wild. Deep buffalo paths showed, leading to salt-licks, though the herds were gone. Deer ranged through glades and thickets. Panthers crouched in tall sycamores. Wildcats were at home there. Black bears crept into hollow trees. Settlers in the new country were buried in corners of the river valleys with cabins far apart, each with a small tract chopped out of the wilderness.

In spite of warring Indians they soon began to raise small surplus crops and to set cattle grazing in the rich silky grass of the meadows. There was a stir, a small bit of trade, as drovers and hunters passed the tavern. Settlers would sometimes gather from a distance of forty miles for a frolic—a dance, with songs, jovial drinking, fighting, and games of marksmanship. Stories were told of encounters with the Indian enemy. Young Davy heard many such tales, and he could decide for himself whether to believe some of them.

A man who stayed one night at the tavern told of a brush with some Indians late one summer's day when he had finished cutting his clover field. He had hung his scythe on a hickory limb and was on his way to the barn for his oxen when one of his dogs growled. He turned and saw some Indians swiftly gathering up his cocks of clover. He knew that if they stole the clover they would probably come back that night and burn his cabin. From the shelter of his

PANTHERS CROUCHED IN TALL SYCAMORES

barn he took aim and picked off one, then four more as they scattered.

Since a few black and copper heads were still popping up among the clover cocks he dashed at them with rifle and scythe. The clover field became a small battlefield. The ground was wet with Indian blood.

"And do you know," said the settler slowly, "the next year a double crop of Indian grass came up with my clover? Every tuft of it was stiff and sharp like an Indian scalplock, and all the clover heads were copper red!"

"Haw!" said a man in a corner, and the ring of laughter went up in the tavern.

Together, Tennessee and Kentucky made a land of marvels. Stories were told of a great race who lived there before the Indians, and of strange caves in the mountains to the west. Many tales were told of curious animals. Huge snapping turtles of western Tennessee were talked about, with shells as big as kegs, heads as big as a boy's head, and a swift snap of the jaws when annoyed. This snapping turtle —the alligator terrapin—became a symbol of the touchy hunter of the West, quick and savage in his own defense.

There was always high talk of hunting and marksmanship. "Why I know a man can nick the edges of a silver shilling at three hundred yards," said a hunter, lounging in front of the tavern.

"I know one that can cut the string of a kite as it flies out of eyesight," said another, "or bring down a wild goose flying."

Overhead in early spring great flocks of gray wild geese

might be seen going north, their long necks with heavy black banding outstretched, far out of range. In the thick of the forest a flock of red and green parroquets would rise suddenly from a tree, startled by Davy's approach, then settled again in a brightly colored shower.

Davy's father let him have a long rifle and a single load and ball and powder when he was eight years old. With this he could go out any day. If he missed, he went without his dinner. Soon he was bringing home a squirrel or possum. Once he slipped away with the rifle and caught sight of a small fat bear cub in a thicket and rashly took aim. A she-bear seemed to rise out of the ground. He knew enough not to prolong the encounter. Holding fast to the heavy rifle, he ran with the angry she-bear after him. The thicket was more favorable to a bear's progress than a boy's and he would probably have been overtaken had not the little cub raised a sharp whining howl. The bear stopped, listened, turned. Davy had his advantage and, reaching an open space, sped away.

The boy was of small use about the tavern, carrying water or holding strangers' horses. His father called him quirky. Out in the forest, when his single round of ammunition was gone, there were always sounds to be listened to—faint rustles, breathings, the cry of birds and small animals. The danger of Indian raids still lingered; all sounds were important. Gradually the boy came to distinguish between many of them, delicately. Soon he was mimicking many birds and small beasts.

When he was not in the forest hunting he was on the

river, paddling a canoe up to the edge of white water where the current might take him over steep falls, then skillfully and suddenly whirling, pushing far upstream, watching for small turtles on the gravelly bottom, sometimes snaring fish. He was hardy and muscular with bold features. His color was high, his eyes and hair dark. In fringed deerskin he looked like a young Indian. He could run like an Indian.

Some hunters were talking as young Davy rode in a canoe, alone on the river.

"That lad could float down all the rivers of Tennessee to the Mississippi, paddling with his hands and an old horn spoon."

"I heard he was cradled in a snapping turtle's shell."

"I heard that cradle had a pair of elk's horns over the top. With an alligator skin over the horns. And a wildcat's skin for a pillow!"

Perhaps this hunter had heard of an infant named Hercules. Or he may have followed his own fancy. In any case labors lay ahead of young Davy that were not much to his liking.

2

A BOY ROAMS OVER THE
MOUNTAINS

THE SUMMER Davy was twelve a German farmer from
the Shenandoah Valley stayed for a night or so at his
father's tavern—one of the many Germans who had settled
in that long curve sheltered by green hills. He had come
to the Tennessee country for cattle, and he wanted a strong
boy to help him drive them on the long journey to his farm

in Virginia, some four hundred miles away. John Crockett was in need of money. For a small sum he bound Davy out to the farmer.

"He's quirky," John Crockett insisted in private warning.

Driving cattle was heavy work, over muddy trails, over rolling hills and the higher mountains, through rivers and streams. The German kept a close watch over the boy during the day and slept at his side at night. There was no chance for him to run off. When they reached the farm in Virginia Davy was given six dollars according to the agreement, but the farmer wanted more of his labor and insisted that he stay and work on the farm. Davy, out of his element, thought that he was obliged to stay.

Commerce between the eastern coast and the new West was carried on mainly by wagoners, who took flour, sugar, barrels of molasses and odd articles into the new country, and returned with corn, rye, and other produce. Wagoners were a rough lot—a race much like the boatmen of the western rivers, banded together in rough and jovial fellowship; there were open-hearted men among them. A few of them passed the German's farm one day whom Davy had seen at his father's tavern, and when they found that he wanted to make the journey to Tennessee, they promised to take him well on the road toward home if he would join them seven miles farther on, where they meant to spend the night.

As good fortune would have it, the farmer and his family were away for a visit. "I gathered my clothes and what little money I had," said Davy, "and put them all together under the head of my bed. Sleep seemed to be a stranger to me, and I felt mighty queer. But so it was, about three hours before day I got up to make my start. I found it was snowing fast, and that the snow was then on the ground about eight inches deep. The whole sky was hid by the falling snow, so that I had to guess my way to the big road. I guided myself by the opening between the timber, and before I overtook the wagons the earth was covered about as deep as my knees. My tracks filled so briskly after me that by daylight my Dutch master would have seen no trace which I left."

He reached the wagoners' camp-fire about an hour before daylight and found them stirring. They shared their breakfast with him, and they all soon set out on the journey west. But Davy was now possessed to be at home; every turn of the wheels seemed slow. On reaching the Roanoke he determined to set out on foot alone. He had traveled only a short distance along the trail by the river when he was overtaken by a gentleman on horseback, leading a horse, who evidently liked the boy's looks or bearing, for he offered to let him ride. Without a horse Davy would have been obliged to swim the cold waters of the river. They forded, and traveled westward over the mountains. It may be that Davy told lively stories of the new country as they jogged on. At last they reached a dark pass from which they could see the long and softly folded valleys that lay within the great valley of the Tennessee spreading out before them, with the rivers silvery, the distances purple as grape, the hills dark now with rain and melted snow.

THEY REACHED A DARK PASS

Descending rapidly, they kept together until they reached a point about fifteen miles from John Crockett's tavern. There the gentleman turned off on the road to Kentucky and the boy went the rest of the way on foot. John Crockett greeted him without surprise.

For a few weeks Davy went to school, but he soon got into a scrape with the schoolmaster and with another lad, and fearing his father's anger, thirsting for more adventure, he slipped away and bound himself out to a drover taking cattle to Virginia. They made the long hard journey eastward over the Blue Ridge and onward to a little town called Front Royal, where the drover sold his cattle and gave Davy a few dollars.

The boy intended to return home, making his way back over the western trail on foot, but he met another of the race of wagoners coming from the West who seemed a jolly sort of fellow, and who persuaded him to turn about and travel north with him to the Maryland border. The wagoner said that when he had left his load he would make up another and return to Tennessee and that Davy might go with him. But at the Maryland border there was no back load for Tennessee. The man decided to go on some miles further in search of one.

Davy, whose money was now spent, hired himself out as a plowboy. The wagoner soon returned but he still lacked the necessary load for the West, so he began hauling loads to Baltimore. Work on a farm was little to Davy's liking, but he stayed through the winter and by spring had earned enough to buy new clothes, with a small sum left over.

Since he had never seen a city he decided to accompany the wagoner on one of his trips to Baltimore, and set out, giving his money to his friend for safekeeping. They hadn't traveled far when the horses took fright and ran away, with Davy riding among the barrels.

"Away they went like they'd seen a ghost. They made a sudden wheel around and broke the wagon tongue slap, short off as a pipe-stem," he said, telling the story afterwards. "And snap went the axletrees at the same time, and of all the flouncing about of flour barrels that ever was seen! I had a chance to be ground up fine as ginger. But if a fellow is born to be hung he will never be drowned," he said grandly, "and I wasn't hurt."

When they entered Baltimore he slipped off for a few moments and hid his bundle under a stone wall, thinking that everyone would know him for a western country boy if he carried it over his shoulder. He then sauntered down to the quay and saw ships with sails flying and so many masts that they looked like a western cane-brake. Baltimore was in its heyday as a port. On the edge of a wharf a ship was lying with some of her canvas loosened, and he stepped aboard. He was met by the captain, who looked him over and saw that he was strong and tall. "How would you like to make a voyage to London?" said he, and told Davy that he was looking for just such a boy. "I'd like it well," said Davy.

The captain asked about his parents and where they lived. When Davy told him that they lived in Tennessee he was even more friendly. Quickly fired by a new ambition, Davy started back into the town to get his bundle.

On the way he ran across the wagoner, who seemed well pleased to learn that Davy was about to set sail for London, and walked with him for some distance, until they came to the stretch of stone wall where the bundle was concealed. As Davy bent down to pick it up the wagoner—a strapping fellow—pinioned his arms behind him with one hand and seized the bundle with the other. Grasping the boy's shoulder, pushing Davy before him, he walked rapidly through the streets.

"Now, my lad, we're going to travel," he said, "and if you cry out I'll give you up and swear you're a bound boy who has fled from his master."

There was some truth in this, for Davy, if not a bound boy, was a runaway. Having been tricked, he was stubbornly silent, and the wagoner kept a close watch over him until the wagon was loaded and they were well on their way to the West again. In Baltimore he had seen only the ships and a glimpse of the Chesapeake, perhaps the outside of a theater, and some gayly dressed men and women on the streets.

At last the habit of moving softly in the forest stood him in good stead. He stole away in the night and in the early morning overtook another wagoner going into the West, to whom he told his story. His new companion insisted upon going back to recover the money which the other had taken for safekeeping. They went. But the man claimed that he hadn't a penny, having spent his own money and Davy's too: so with his new friend the boy started along the road.

With the heavy load travel was slow, and again the boy found himself in sudden haste to return home. One night he stayed at a place where a number of wagoners were encamped, and when Davy spoke of his intention of going on ahead the company made up a little purse of three dollars for him so that he might have money for food on his journey.

At the little hamlet of Montgomery Court House in Virginia this sum gave out. In the distance he could see the peaks of the Blue Ridge; after so many mishaps it seemed that he was never to return to Tennessee. He went to work for a farmer and earned a little money, but not enough to take him home. Winter had set in. He bound himself out to a hatter, hoping to earn a handsome sum. For eighteen months he worked in the hatter's shop though the finicking work was little to his taste. Davy, who had worn only a cap of fox or coonskin in the wilderness, now brushed beaver for tall hats which fashionable gentlemen in the cities would wear. This venture came to nothing, for the hatter became involved in debt and left the country. Davy received nothing for his time, and possessed now only some badly worn clothes.

He took work on farms as he could catch it, and after several months accumulated enough money to buy clothing, with a small sum left over to carry him on the way home.

When he reached the New River it was autumn, with

stormy weather. The water was white, seething, and very high; no one was willing to take him across. Here his adventures on the western streams stood him in good stead. He found a canoe and started out alone. But he had never paddled on a river so wild as this one. "When I got out on the river I would have given the world, if it had belonged to me, to be back on shore," he said, telling the story. "But there was no time to lose. I turned the canoe across the waves, and to do this I had to turn it nearly up the river, as the wind came from that way, and I went two miles before I could land."

The canoe was half full of water when he reached the shore, and the clothes he wore were nearly frozen. He was obliged to walk more than three miles before he could find a house or a fire at which to warm himself. He set out again the next day, but the journey was still hard. He had so little money that he had to spend it sparingly for food, and he slept in such cold corners as he could find.

Over the Blue Ridge the trail was lonely, and there was always the chance of encounters with rough characters. At night he was alone, a young straggling boy for all his strength and wit and will, finding a place for himself under a ledge or a fallen tree. Once when he had gone far aside from the trace to avoid a caravan of wagons he discovered some holes, and making a snare of a reach of grapevine, caught a rabbit. As he built his fire with a bit of flint in a sheltered hollow he could hear the wagoners singing, laughing, calling as they rolled down the mountain. At last, keeping to himself for all the rest of his journey, he reached the dark familiar gap through which he would see the wide spread of the Tennessee country.

At the tavern he found a traveler or two in the bar room, and he withdrew to a corner. Thin and tired, he was now much taller than when he had left; he had been gone nearly three years. No one recognized him.

In the taverns of the West strangers were under suspicion until their intentions and character became reasonably clear. "Light, stranger, and come in," was the friendly word for any rider, but western people, living in lonely places, relished explanations, and most travelers were willing to talk—to talk steadily for an hour or more without interruption, about themselves, their business, about people they had seen on the way, about the weather, and the shortcomings of the government.

A stranger was expected to make himself known. So Davy, sitting quietly in a corner, was closely watched. At last one of his sisters edged toward him, closer and closer, touched him on the arm and said, "This is David."

On the whole David's adventures in the eastern country seemed to command little attention in the Crockett household. John Crockett, always short of funds, at once made a proposal.

"Then you can go on your own hook," he said, ending his plea. He owed a neighbor a considerable sum of money and he was begging this tall boy of his to work for the man until the debt was paid.

For nearly a year Davy worked for the neighbor, and paid the debt. At the end of his time John Crockett declared that he owed money to a Quaker in the neighborhood. Forgetting his original bargain with Davy—that he could go his own way when the first debt was paid—he begged him to clear this debt as well. The boy good-naturedly bound himself out to the Quaker, to work until he had earned the full sum. He worked hard, though he detested farm work, and the Quaker, who was a kindly man, liked him.

When the debt was paid Davy remained on the well-ordered farm. For the first time in his life he had plain neat clothes, and for a few months during the winter the Quaker sent him to school. This gave him the only formal schooling he ever had, and at the time he regarded his efforts in this direction as of small importance.

3

ALONG THE RIVERS

WHEN the grain was reaped and flax pulled there were frolics in the neighborhood, and this lively stripling was warmly welcomed at such gatherings. "Nobody can dance longer or sing longer or get into more scrapes than that lad of Crockett's," said a neighbor.

The Quaker did not approve of these gayeties. "Thee'd best stay at home," he told Davy. "Thee's bound to be a rolling stone, I fear, for all that thee can bend thy back and work hard. Thee's as mettlesome as my bay mare."

One night Davy let himself down from his attic by a

thick strand of grapevine, and borrowed the bay mare, and went to a frolic. All his life he was a dancer; one of the last glimpses we have of him is at a dancing party at a little frontier post in Texas, where he footed it gayly with some charming ladies. The dances of the day were bold and free, but young Crockett's tall figure must have had a sturdy grace, for someone who saw him said that he when he bowed before a certain pretty girl he bent like a young sapling swept by the south wind.

The two were partners in the dances, and Davy believed from what the girl said before the evening was over that she would be willing to marry him. A few days later he walked at evening several miles to the cabin where she lived. She was not to be seen in the clearing as he came up. Instead, a knot of men was gathered there, talking. Among them was the girl's father. David did not wish to make his errand known in so many words so he asked, "Has anybody here seen a bay filly?"

The men guffawed, and someone told him that the fickle young woman had ridden away to Kentucky with a man she had married the day before. Davy walked away speechless, and decided that he was born only for misery.

But he had perfected his skill with the rifle in the few years since he had returned to Tennessee, and it happened that only a few days before he had been lucky at a shooting match. To watch his neat and dexterous movements as he handled his hunting tools was to watch a skilled craftsman. He would quickly blow through the rifle barrel to make sure that it was clear, glance at his flint and thrust a feather through the touch-hole. With a turn of the wrist and fingers he put in a bullet and filled the powder pan. His long, flexible lift of the gun, his easy swift aim, and the accommodating drop of the rifle as he fired seemed a single curving movement. He had already walked away with many small prizes in the neighborhood. This time a prime beef had been offered at a match, and David, shooting from longer and longer distances, had shot against a crowd of older men of the neighborhood. He had ended by winning the whole beef and had sold it for five dollars in gold. He was seldom low-spirited for long, and he still had the money, which seemed a little fortune. As he thought of it and considered the hundred agreeable things for which it might be spent, his spirits rose.

He forgot about the girl who had jilted him, and when another frolic was announced he was earliest on the ground. There was to be a great reaping and flax pulling, and all the young men and women from clearings for miles around were to gather for the work. The frolic was to follow.

The day began with yellow sunlight pouring down and only enough wind to stir the grain in gentle waves. David joined the reapers; the songs of the men and boys could be heard rising above the swish of the reap-hooks. In another field the girls were pulling flax, vying with each other to see who would finish soonest. When the grain was cut and stacked the men strolled over to the flax field. Each chose a girl and helped her end her task. Each pair then became partners for the frolic. David chose a fair-haired, blue-eyed girl named Polly Finley.

Negro slaves made the music at the frolics, thrumming a banjo or playing an old fiddle, shaking the bones, calling the tunes and changes of step. Some of them sat in the corner of the cabin at the reaping party, singing to fiddle-tunes. The bones sounded a quick rat-tat-tat that set every foot shaking, and a few of the company led out, with the rest joining in the chorus of the song. But the great swing of the party was not within the cabin. All soon were out of doors where bran of Indian meal had been strewn over the ground to make it smooth, and tall trees formed shadowy walls. Pitch-pine torches cast a thick yellow light.

The figures of the girls were not squeezed in fashion's mold, nor were their feet encased within the light prunella. Most of the company were barefoot. All wore homespun. They danced as though they would never tire. Play-party songs like "Sell the Thimble" and "Grind the Bottle" and "We're on the Way to Baltimore" were sung and danced. Davy knew the way to Baltimore well, but this was a pleasanter journey than the one he had taken. The dance was wild and irregular, with slow and measured steps for the line of the chorus—

> We're on our way to Baltimore,
> With two behind and two before,
> Around, around, around we go,
> Where oats, peas, beans, and barley grow,
> In   waiting   for   somebody.
>
> 'Tis thus the farmer sows his seed,
> Folds his arms and takes his ease,

Stamps his feet, and claps his hands,
Wheels around, and thus he stands,
In   waiting   for   somebody.

Some of the boys and girls had picked up steps from the
Negroes and could dance the double shuffle and the double
trouble. Reels from Scotland and Ireland were played and
sung in new keys with new words.

With his young partner Davy was quick at the lively
steps. The pair was readiest when the turns were called,
loudest in the singing. They danced the night through, and
when Davy climbed to the Quaker's attic at dawn he was
betrothed to Polly Finley and he was sure this time there
was to be no mistake.

He was now past eighteen. Marriages took place early in
the new country. His own people were willing to have him
marry. To set himself up for farming he bargained with the
Quaker's son to purchase a horse, for which he was to work
six months.

Toward the end of this time, when the marriage papers
had been drawn and the infare for the bride arranged at
John Crockett's tavern, Mrs. Finley declared that Davy
should not have her daughter. She would give no reason.

Davy turned to the girl. "I'll come to you next Thursday
on horseback, leading a horse," he told her squarely, "and
you must be ready to go with me."

The following Thursday he set out with two of his
brothers and their wives, and two young men who were to
be his waiters at the wedding. When they came to the Fin-

leys' cabin they found Mrs. Finley as unwilling as ever to let her daughter go. But the girl's father—who is said to have been descended from the house of Macbeth—firmly gave his consent. The parson was sent for, the wedding took place. Afterwards at John Crockett's there was a great infare or wedding frolic to receive the bride.

Later Mrs. Finley explained that she had only dreaded to lose her daughter. In a fine good humor she gave the pair two cows and two calves. This was a small marriage portion, but Polly's wheel and loom were added, and Polly was a good weaver. The Quaker gave David a substantial order at the store for such things as his wife could use. Davy rented a small farm, and in little or no time Polly Crockett had woven a fine web of cloth and had it ready to make up.

"She's good at that," Davy boasted, "and at pretty near everything else a woman can do."

They lived for some years in a small cabin on a rented farm, but farming was less than ever to young Crockett's taste. He complained that he could never make a fortune that way. He hunted, but now the country round about the Holston was becoming too well settled for wild life. Stone houses had been built, and men often came over the eastern mountains in fine chaises. The road to Knoxville was steadily traveled.

Davy and Polly soon had two little boys. "I want my boys to grow up in new country," said Davy, "and learn to hunt. I want to hunt myself. It's best to be gone."

He resolved to take up wild land in the Duck and Elk

River country, over the Cumberland Mountains in southern Tennessee.

"Thee's going to roll," said the Quaker when he heard this news, "as I said. Thee'll never make a farmer, I fear, but perhaps thee'll become the greatest hunter in the West." Davy smiled and said he couldn't change his mind.

In the spring he packed a few pieces of household gear on two well-grown colts. Polly and the two little boys rode the old horse, and with Davy and a pair of dogs on foot the family set out early for a point on the Holston where they would take passage on a flatboat. This was the river country of the West, and most men traveled by the rivers when they could.

Arks, broadhorns, flatboats—each of these names was given them—might now be seen on the smaller streams as well as on the Ohio and the Mississippi. Travel by flatboat was the easiest way of pushing into new country where there were no roads and when trails were what they were often called—traces. The boats, of rough planking, were sometimes a hundred feet in length and could carry several families of settlers, with their horses, cattle, chickens, sheep, and gear. Long beech oars were set in the square bow, each manned by two or more boatmen. A broad cabin was planted in the middle of the deck, and a tall crotched pole was fastened against its rear, reaching well above the flat roof. Through this another long oar slanted down over the square stern into the water and was used as a rudder by two or three boatmen standing on the roof, where they could see every turn and riffle of the stream.

On the river Polly and Davy met other young settlers, going like themselves into wild land. The red-shirted riverboatmen kept up a running repartee with men ashore or on other boats along the river. Like the wagoners they consorted together, had their own lingo, their own way of bantering, their wit, which was quick, and their songs, which were both rowdy and sentimental. Thousands of them were now afloat on the western rivers, noisy, quarrelsome, full of sport, gathering for short holidays at taverns when a journey was ended, and then away again up or down the rivers.

The waters of the Holston were high in spring, and it was a perilous affair to steer the heavy craft over riffles and chutes and around sharp bends. A collision of flatboats on a rapidly running stream was the danger. On rounding a bend the steersmen would blow great wooden staved horns, whose soft, melancholy notes were loved and remembered by many who traveled along the western rivers.

On open easy water the boatmen would sing out—

> "Hard upon the beech oar!
> She moves too slow!"

The air was full of boatmen's songs and full of talk. Flatboats passed, plying the rivers as shops or "doggeries," drawing alongside the arks to sell food or spirits or fancy notions to travelers.

Small empty boats made their way upstream, "bushwhacking." A boatman in the bow would seize a bush or the branch of a willow tree on the bank and then, holding fast to this would walk toward the stern. Another boatman quickly followed, seizing a bush, then another, and another, making a line that walked to the stern, holding fast to the bushes. Around to the bow they went and again seized bushes or branches one after another, holding fast to them and again walking to the stern and around to the bow. Slowly the heavy craft moved upstream and the steersman kept the boat true. Large boats were broken up for lumber at the end of the long voyages down the Ohio and the Mississippi to New Orleans.

The Holston poured into the broad silver Tennessee, and then there were many winding miles to the southwest through fresh spring weather, past grassy valleys and open glades, past glinting stands of red maple, persimmon, tall sweet gum, and broad chestnut. The ark on which the Crocketts were traveling skirted rocky spurs of the Cumberlands. At last the Tennessee crossed a trail that ran crookedly over the mountains and down into the Elk River country.

Here the Crocketts' gear was packed again on the two colts, and Polly mounted the old horse with the little boys. Davy was on foot, the dogs alongside, and the journey was made over a rough steep trail, wet with spring rains. The vistas were fine and far, the mountainside rosy with laurel. Maypops could be found in the woods, and fresh wild ginger.

Davy bought a little clearing at the head of the Mulberry Fork of the Elk River. He had come in time for planting, and in putting up his small, windowless cabin he had the

THE WATERS OF THE HOLSTON WERE HIGH

help of other settlers who came, sometimes from a distance, to help with log-rolling. The cabin had an earthen floor and a clay fireplace across one end. Later Crockett expected to have bearskins for rugs.

Many settlers thereabouts had never seen a carpet. A Virginian had come into this region, built a puncheon floor for his cabin, and laid a carpet over it. He invited the neighbors in for a treat. They looked at his carpet and thought it was a bed quilt spread down to make a show. "It's naught but a piece of pride," they said severely among themselves.

Bears were to be had in this region, though not in great enough numbers to please Crockett. The country had been hunted for years by the Indians, some of whom still lived there, and white men had also raided the forests. But wild turkeys were to be had, and possums and raccoons.

A few coonskins over a hunter's shoulder were like money jingling in his pocket. A pair of them was worth a quarter, and a dozen pairs could be traded for flour and sugar.

Raccoons were fond of turtle's eggs, and in summer they would look for traces made by soft shelled turtles as the turtles crawled over the sandy bottom of some quiet little creek. Stealthily the wary coons would follow these traces, walking along the banks, until they discovered the eggs. Leaning over the clear water of a little stream or branch they would swiftly scoop up tadpoles with their paws. Troops of them would swiftly and quietly raid the cornfields, finding the sweet milky young ears.

In autumn when the woodpiles were larger than the

cabins and the frost glimmered white, when the corn was still on the stalk though its blades were dry or gone, they prowled out of the woods at night, their eyes shining like emeralds. Neat, wise, swift, they would climb the corn-stalks, bending, breaking them, rapidly feasting on the yellow ears, making for the woods at the slightest rustle within the cabin or at the sound of a dog stirring.

On spring mornings that other thief, the possum, haunted the little streams or branches that flowed through deep forests into the Mulberry Creek, looking for delicious morsels, young frogs, or pokeberry, or young nettle, and listening for the morning call of the wild turkey. It was the female's answer he wanted. Slipping toward her and following her to the nest, waiting for hours sometimes until she left it, he would gain a chance to suck the eggs. Sly as a drop of snow, the possum was as great a thief around the clearing as the coon. Eggs in the henhouse were his plunder, and in autumn he topped off a good meal with grapes and ripe persimmons.

It was when the persimmons were in their most delicious state and the frost lay white on the ground that the wily possum, after so many succulent meals, himself became most excellent eating. Roast possum tasted like young suckling pig.

Alone with his dogs or sometimes joining with one or two other hunters, Crockett was more often in the forests than on his little farm. The dogs would pick up a scent and with their bell voices rolling would be gone through the woods, the clear notes of the hunting horn urging them on.

Young Crockett could raise his own strong voice in a high call that floated far through the air and roused the dogs as keenly as the horn. Hunters said that he knew how to throw his voice so that it would follow his dogs along the ground between ridges of the hills, and that his hunting call could travel even round the shoulder of a steep bluff.

Then would come the deep, full, insistent baying of the dogs. "Treed!" Crockett would cry and be off full swing through woods and bottom land.

The scent was not always hot. Sometimes there were so many traces of it as to confuse the dogs, for wary raccoons would circle and cut in on their own tracks to throw them off. When dogs were barking up a great oak the coon could slip into the upper branches where leaves hung thick, and it was a puzzle to find him with his rings and stripes as he lay curled round the farther side of a limb. But Crockett was long-sighted, sure of aim, ready to guess what a coon would do.

"Crockett can outsmart most any coon or possum," his neighbors said.

He soon had enough coonskins to barter for provisions at the neighboring doggery and enough sweet possum meat to keep his boys round and fat.

Hunting far into the forests he shot an occasional black bear, so when winter came jerked bear meat hung from the rafters of the little cabin. The corn pone was full of cracklings, with wild honey eaten with it for a treat, gathered before winter set in. In winter there were plenty of warm fox furs for caps, deerskin for leggings, coonskins for coats and furs to pile on the beds at night.

Quail and wild pigeons Crockett never hunted. "Since I was a little boy," he said, "I never did shoot a bird. Birds are trifling—except wild turkeys."

A fine wild gobbler stood nearly four feet high, with wide velvety black satin breast and small white turban cap, a great breadth and spread of tail—bronze, purple and gold —the gorgeously colored head lifted erect when alarmed or curious, the small clear hazel eyes showing bright. Hunting wild turkeys meant matching wits with the wariest creatures of the forest. Wild turkeys were so shy that some hunters never saw them and thought that they had been driven from the woods by the arrival of the settlers. Only their light footprints in the dust of a path or in soft soil beside a creek showed that they still belonged to this region. In a hard winter when they were all but starved, they would pass by a wealth of scattered grain over a trap. So cautious were the gobblers that even when their mates called they would listen as if they were trying out every quaver, every half tone to make sure they were not deceived. They might not answer at all, or only with a single small muffled note.

It was with the call of the female bird that hunters tried to lure the great gobblers. Crockett would set out alone with his gun and a turkey call made from a bone of a turkey's wing or a bit of wood with a nail driven through it. Scraping this with a stone or blowing through it, he could imitate the small cry of the fledglings if he liked, or the love-notes of the female, or even her soft throaty gurgle as she found a tempting bit of food. He was now a master mimic; he could imitate the sound of any wild creature so that its mates in the forest would stop and listen. He could play so craftily on his turkey-bone that even the wary gobbler would at last hesitate, listen and perhaps answer, and finally be drawn toward the bit of brush or wood from which the notes arose.

During a whole long morning he might see no sign of a turkey. Then toward noon he might catch a slight sound from a distance, a sound which even to other hunters might seem like innumerable small sounds of the forest.

"That might be a woodpecker trying to yawn, or it might—" A good hunter knew it was the faint, very distant cluck of a turkey gobbler. The sound might be repeated, still in the distance. Crockett would find a place behind a fallen tree with a thatch of green leaves before him through which he placed the muzzle of his gun; he waited. At last with his turkey call he would give a single answering soft cluck, so quietly that the sound fell in with all the quiet sounds of the forest.

Half a mile away a gobbler would start, every feather instantly in place, rising in bronze and purple glory to his full height. An intensely curious bird, he would listen. Hearing nothing, he might at last begin to trot over the ground, looking for food. Again that soft tempting cluck would reach him. Starting suddenly forward, he would answer. There would be no reply; a skilled turkey hunter knew the ways of his quarry too well to call again immediately. A slow hour might pass. Finally impatient, the bird might give a positive *cluck,* and ten minutes later hear the low reply. If really aroused he would now press forward at full speed, half running, half flying, yet stopping cautiously from time to time, distracted by half a dozen pleasures. A little branch whose waters were deep and still might bring him to a halt. Wild turkeys were vain as peacocks, and he might parade up and down before the branch as before a mirror, back and forth, back and forth, more and more slowly. Or he might start looking for insects as though nothing were more important. Or he might be flightily upset by the rustle of a cricket or some other small sound. There would be long pauses as he picked his way about in underbrush: then that *cluck*.

The gobbler suddenly opened his beak wide and rolled forth a loud, satisfying answer. He crossed the stream in bold flight. He stopped cautiously from time to time, it is true, with his long neck outstretched, his bright eyes peering, but on he went until he came to an open space. Then another of his pleasures brought him to a pause. The sun rather than the mirroring stream attracted him. A turkey loves the sun, and will stand for hours in bright light. It seemed now that this great gobbler was to preen his fine feathers until sundown.

Several hundred yards away, out of gunshot, was the fallen tree and thicket where Crockett lay flat on the ground, his gun at his shoulder, looking in his worn leather clothes like a dead log. He hardly winked. At last the turkey tired of the sun, and with a long memory returned to his original errand. He gobbled—gobbled loudly. Crockett gave a long soft enticing *cluck*. This was the test of his art, with the turkey so close. The gobbler began proudly to strut. His plumage unfolded, his wattles grew scarlet. His gorgeous bronze and purple tail rose and opened in a great fan; his fine head glittered in rainbow tints. On he came with a hitching gait, glowing in the sunshine. On he came—slowly, still not within gunshot. He paused—looked about with suspicion; then he came forward with a bold sure movement, advancing toward his final goal, as a turkey hunter said, "like a gay horse toward the music of a drum or a fine ship beating against the wind."

In the stillness Crockett could hear the brush of wings over the ground. At the last the turkey moved into range. There was a shot.

Even with the soft perfection of his call and a long patience—which Crockett did not enjoy—the great bird might come within half a dozen yards of his range and a squirrel would suddenly dash down a tree with a rattle of twigs. Wheeling quickly, the turkey would be off at a furious speed, tail down, feathers flat, running and flying through brush and trees, over streams, far into some deep thicket from which he was not to be drawn again that day.

4

WHEN HUNTERS MEET

I ONCE hunted after the same old gobbler for three years and never saw him three times," said an old hunter at a tavern on the Elk River some miles below Crockett's cabin. A group had gathered, with Crockett among them. Hunters would come from long distances for stories and talk. With all the perils and long labor of the hunt for game, theirs was a leisurely life. Often at the taverns there were travelers to whom it was interesting to tell stories.

The old hunter went on. "I knew that gobbler's call the way I know the call of Music, my old deer dog, and his track was as plain to me as the trail of a tree hauled along a dusty road. I hunted him always in the same range and about the same scratchin's, and he got so when I gave my turkey-call he would slip around looking for my foot tracks and then run in the opposite direction.

"The old feller kept a good deal to a ridge, and at the end of this where it went down into a swamp was a hollow cypress tree. It was a good place to lie in wait for a turkey. I was determined to outwit him, so one day I put on my shoes heels foremost, and walked leisurely down the ridge that way, and got into that hollow cypress and gave my call. It would of done you good to see that old gobbler a coming towards me on the trot, a looking sharp at my tracks and a thinking I had gone in the opposite direction. I got him."

There was a meditative pause.

"Ever hear about Zip Spooner and the big black bear down in the patch of tall grass?" said Crockett. "This is true enough. 'Twas toward dusk, and the bear took to a branch that was running high and was swollen and rapid. Zip had nothing but his hunting knife with him, so he cut down an oak sapling, and took after the bear. The bear turned on him in the middle of the branch with all his teeth a gnashing, but Zip pushed at him with the sapling and the bear scrambled out on the other side and went up a high oak.

"Now Zip's pretty smart, and he took a big stone and began hitting the foot of the tree as if he was cutting it down, and by this time his dogs had come up. But the bear was smart too. He slipped out to the end of a limb and gathered himself up into a ball and dropped. He was a big old bear, fat as a candle, and he bounced up several feet right over the heads of the dogs and then dropped and was off. But the dogs was on his trail and they treed him.

"Then Zip began with the stone at the foot of *that* tree as if he was cutting it down, and the bear slipped to the end of a limb again and dropped. He bounced right up over those dogs and was off. I swear that old bear went out on a limb and bounced over those dogs three times. At last they all got down near the river, and into it galloped the old bear with the dogs after him, but an ark came along with a great push of water and noise, and the bear ducked in among the waves and shoved around and made land again somewhere down the shore, and the dogs lost him."

"A bear's smart's a man," said the turkey hunter.

"Down my way, Davy Crockett," said a lone traveler from Mississippi, "we heard about the ghost of an old bear *you* killed."

"Roundabout here they said they saw him," Crockett answered, "so out we piled one night to find him. 'There he is, Davy, there he is,' they said. So I went up to the tree and sure enough there looked to be a bear in the hollow of it. But when I cracked my knuckles together the old ghost was gone."

"Gone!" echoed a man from the Mississippi Territory.

"I wish I may be shot if he weren't gone! Take my eyes for green grog bottles if there was anything left but a barked tree with two big knot holes in it for eyes!"

"Maybe you grinned at him," said a hunter. "We heard you could grin most any varmint right out of countenance."

How the stories arose as to Davy Crockett's grin nobody knows. There were many of them. Perhaps some story-teller who had talked of giants with great strength and a strange grin somehow attached the grin to Crockett. But there is another explanation. Most of the stories had Davy grinning at a coon—grinning like a possum at his old enemy the coon. He sometimes told these stories about himself.

"I tried grinnin' not long ago," said Davy. "You know there's an old coon that's been round over yonder for a long time, raiding everybody's cornfield and doubling four times on his tracks whenever the hunt's up. He'd get the dogs a barking round the tree, then slip over the branches to another tree and get away and leave 'em there. If there's anything meaner than an old coon dog barkin' up the wrong tree I don't know what it is.

"Well, I saw a coon in the topmost crotch of an oak as I was coming home one night, and I was sure it was that rascally old one. It was moony and clear, and I thought I wouldn't shoot him down but I would grin him down. So I grinned and grinned, and there he sat looking more like an old coon every minute with his stripes and rings. He was a ringtailed roarer sure enough. I got into a pretty savage humor when he didn't fall, so at last I clomb the oak, but"—he said gravely—"it was nothing but a knothole, 'thout any bark on it."

A Yankee traveler had joined the group to hear the talk, but there was a long pause.

"Lay low, stranger," said Crockett to the Yankee, "and perhaps you'll see some fun."

Two Negroes had come in to light the bear oil lamps and were humming a sturdy little tune. Crockett gave a turkey call. Others followed with calls, soft and loud. The room was full of clucks and gobbling. The pair of Negroes answered, gobbling, and began bending and strutting, leaning down to pick up something from the ground as a turkey picks up grains of corn, rising again on tiptoe. Keeping the tune and the strutting, they shuffled some dance steps.

"Ever see our catfish?" said Crockett to the Yankee. "Blue Cat, White Cat, Mud Cat, Yellow Cat. Weigh a hundred pounds and dance you all over the rivers of the West if you get 'em on the line. Smart as a man and sometimes smarter."

The darkeys sang out—

"Met Mr. Catfish a comin' down stream,
Says Mr. Catfish, 'What does you mean?'
Caught Mr. Catfish by de snout,
An' turned Mr. Catfish wrong side out."

For a moment Crockett fell in lustily with the wild steps.

"Have a horn," he said to the Yankee as the song ended and they all crowded into the bar. The tavern keeper brought them brimming horns.

"When does the moon get a horn?" asked a hunter.

"Whenever she gets a quarter," said Crockett.

"I never see a quarter," said a little man mournfully. "All I've got is coonskins. But furs is money, and coonskins is good if you've got enough of 'em." He threw a pair down on the counter and bought another horn.

"Let's snuff the candle," said a hunter when many horns had been drunk.

Out went the whole crowd into the clearing beside the tavern. A Negro boy carried a lighted candle to the crotch of a tree and set it up there. A tow-headed man stepped back into the shadow with his gun.

"You've put it out," roared the crowd as he took aim and shot.

The Negro boy ran forward with another smoking candle.

"Watch Crockett! Crockett! Crockett can do it," shouted the men. His skill at this difficult game was famous.

"No slang-whanging," said Crockett. Taking quick and easy aim, he snuffed the candle with a shot, leaving the flame burning brightly. Another smoking candle was put up, and he moved to a farther distance and shot, snuffing this, then again from a more distant point, each time neatly trimming the wick, leaving the flame.

The shooting-match continued for an hour by the light of torches as the hunters shot at buttons, ribbons, at the tip of a fox's tail—pinning this to a tree.

Crockett began notching the edge of a circle of tin with one shot after another at three hundred feet.

Suddenly a distant murmuring sound was heard. He paused. The whole crowd stood motionless. A thick haze had overspread the trees and the river, and a long oval yellowish spot was rising from the West. A wind struck the tallest trees, bending the highest branches to the ground. In a moment the whole forest was swirling and turning, bending, breaking. Trees writhed and snapped and were borne through the air like a cloud of feathers. The sound was like a giant waterfall, and the clearing was piled high with a rush of trees. Great branches struck the tavern. It was all over in a moment.

"Hurricane!" someone shouted.

Crockett was running toward his cabin, a few miles away.

The rim of the hurricane had passed it, sweeping off the roof. The solid timbers stood awry. The clay chimney was partly torn off at the top and riven through the center. When Crockett arrived Polly was calmly walking up and down and the little boys were playing on the floor.

"These things sometimes comes in pairs," said Davy, "or an earthquake may follow. We'll sleep outside. It's safer. I can curl up close as a rattlesnake, or lay out straight as a gum log on the ground, and I expect my little boys to do the same." They picked up some furs and lay down in the open space before the cabin.

There was no earthquake, and no other hurricane, and Crockett's corn was still standing. But the timbers of the cabin had to be straightened, the roof replaced.

"I don't believe we'll stay here anyway," Crockett told his wife. "There's getting to be most too much of a hotchpotch of people roundabout, and I crave to go where there's wilder land and more game. Over south near the mountains there's good soil in the thick of hunting country and I think I'd like it well there. From all signs there's going to be an early harvest. Soon as harvest's over I'll ride yonder and build a cabin, then come back, and we'll take our plunder and move. We've been here most two years anyway."

Polly was willing to go. Davy sold his patch of land for fifty dollars—a fair sum—and bought a small tract near a deep stream in the forest. Before winter set in he had moved there with his family and his dogs and no more plunder than the horses could carry. The new cabin was near the boundary of the Mississippi Territory.

In this deeper forest panthers lurked, robbing the hunter of the deer he had killed if he was not watchful, attacking men if startled close at hand. A settler in this region was walking up and down in his cabin with a child in his arms one evening. The door was open, and as he turned away from it a panther slipped in. The door was slammed shut by a sudden wind, the man turned quickly, the panther crouched and sprang. The settler dropped the child and slid to the floor so as to get the beast under him, and by a sudden wrench succeeded in turning so that he could seize the panther by the throat. The strong grasp loosened the animal's hold, and with a ferocious strength the settler rose and hurled him into the wide fireplace where a great pile of hickory logs was burning. Choked and blinded by smoke, singed by the fire, the panther ran up the chimney, out on the roof, leapt, and fled.

49

"I've seen as many as three painters crouched on trees near that big salt lick way over yonder," Crockett told Polly. "They was waiting to spring on the deer that come there. This morning I'd just sighted a fine buck in that far timber when I saw a painter on the limb above. I got the painter and we'll have the skin, but I lost my deer."

There were wildcats too in this country, with a look on their faces like that of a rattlesnake, with eyes shining like fire as they stared down from the branches of a tree at a pack of dogs and a hunter, their ears pressed to their heads and hair angrily upraised.

"Wildcats can move over dried leaves or twigs as quiet as the breath of the morning wind," said Crockett, "as they steal and they hunt."

They stole from rabbits' burrows, from the poultry yard, they hunted coons and possums and squirrels in the high trees, ascending to their tops as lightly as a bird, then droping with their prey to the ground with the softness of a feather. The turkey hunter, at last luring a great gobbler almost within range of his gun, might see a wildcat creeping like a serpent through the grasses. If he shot the cat the turkey was lost. If he lay still the cat got the turkey.

With sharp hearing that seized every sound, stealing over the ground in moccasins, Crockett would lurk on the ridges where wild turkeys ran, sometimes bringing down a great bird, sometimes bagging a wildcat instead, desirable only for the warm fine skin. Farther and farther into the mountains and into wild land he hunted, often bringing back deer and bear.

WHEN HUNTERS MEET

Once he saw some Indians in a canoe armed with knives, making for a bear that was swimming across the river. The bear swam calmly on, making no great effort to escape. When the canoe came up with him he flung about, thrust his big paws over the side of it, and in spite of the Indians' knives turned his enemies with a quick somersault into the water. He swam off as calmly as he had started nor did any Indian swim after him to risk a slap of the great paws.

Only a few scattered settlers and hunters belonged to this region. Now and again traders came, solitary figures riding over the mountains on an old nag, sometimes tramping it, bringing notions and fancy goods to sell at the tavern or the doggery down the river, or to trade for furs. Crockett would choose from the trader's pack a few trinkets for Polly.

Occasionally a traveler from far parts to the east or north would appear, exploring the new country with a wise eye. Crockett and the other hunters did not welcome these visitors. Newspapers published in the cities from which such travelers came were sometimes carried into the deepest wilderness, and those who could would spell out what they said. In these sheets were often found jokes and quips about the backwoodsmen, which they did not relish.

One of these travelers had learned of Crockett's skill as a hunter from his friends in the Elk River country and came to his cabin. Crockett gave him the best food at the table, the softest furs at night. The stranger insisted that he wished to be taken hunting, speaking in what Crockett regarded as a lofty manner. So Crockett led him southward toward the Indian country into an old forest so dense that even at noonday the sun hardly penetrated there. Hurricanes had passed through long before, leaving dead tree trunks stripped of their branches and whitening with ghostly age. Grapevines larger than a man's body crept for some distance along the ground, then suddenly sprang a hundred feet into the air and wound themselves around the dense top of some giant tree.

In the midst of this forest Crockett and the stranger camped for the night, taking turns in keeping the fire high, hearing the panther's scream, seeing the blaze of the wildcat's eyes.

"He *thought* he saw a wildcat's eyes," said Crockett to a little group of hunters at the doggery. "Maybe it was foxfires but that stranger didn't know the difference. Maybe it was owls he heard. Anyway it seemed to me that all the owls in all creation was out. We had a high night of it. I tell you he came out of that forest as white as a hickory ash heap. He had a rifle but I could see by the way he carried it he was no hunter. Why, he knew no more about handling a rifle than a goose knows about rib stockings, and anyhow I led him into a part of the forest where there's hardly ever any game. But maybe he'll have something to put in the papers now. Maybe he'll write a book!"

"It was pretty strange in that old forest," he went on, "strange enough for anybody when all is said and done. There's some marvelous wonderful things in this great garden of Tennessee. Why, I know an even more curious place, though bless me if I'm sure I could find it again.

"One morning old Whirlwind, my lead dog, and I were

oing through the forest up toward the mountains on a long
unt and there came up a rainstorm. We felt a low soft
vind coming toward us over the ground and soon we came
o the mouth of a cave. The wind came out of it like a
•reath. The storm was coming on heavier and heavier, so
n we went, and the first thing I saw was some white bones
et all around. Whirlwind acted strange. I went up to them
nd found it was a whole lot of skulls piled high—Indian
kulls, I reckon.

"Whirlwind said never a word but he looked right at me
nd I looked at him. I knowed what Whirlwind was think-
ng of. He was wondering how they come there, and I
ouldn't tell him. But there are stranger things than that
n caves up in Kentucky. There's a deep river running
hrough one of them, and alligators stay there, which proves
hat the river must run underground till it comes to the old
Mississippi. There's snakes too, and blind fish that leap out
of the water. A man told me that was there, and he said he
knowed they was blind yet he thought they stared at him.

"Owls and bats there are in plenty, and foxfires, and way
>ack in the cave there's silver branches hanging down. I'd
ike to see it but I wouldn't want to take old Whirlwind,
or he had enough right down here in Tennessee. He shiv-
:red and shook, and I thought myself that the storm might
>e better than the cave, so out we went, and the long breath
vas still a blowing out of it when we went into the rain."

"There's a story they was giants here once," said a hunter.

"There's Indians right here now," said another, "and
hey're going to give us a heap of trouble."

5

THE INDIAN FIGHTER

NEWS traveled mysteriously in the new West. At times
no tangible means of communication seemed to exist yet among a few scattered cabins set deep in the wilderness events would be told that had happened hundreds of
miles away.

Suddenly a name was said—Tecumseh, echoing among
the thickly wooded valleys of southern Tennessee. With the
name came word that the Indians were gathering for re-
sistance against the whites.

Gradually the Indian peoples had retreated as hunters
and settlers had penetrated far into the new country, but
no one could think that they had left willingly. The Cherokees, the Creeks, the Choctaws, had occupied this beautiful
land for generations. Their ancestors were buried there.

54

They were obliged to leave behind their favorite hunting grounds, their well-built towns and villages. Unlike the tribes of the far western plains, these Indians preferred not to roam. And they were proud, knowing well the history of their own race, accomplished in many arts, possessing rich ceremonials. A clash on a large scale was inevitable as they found that even the new lands to which they had retreated were being invaded by the Americans.

Tecumseh was a Shawanoe, born at the ancient seat of his tribe in the valley of the Miami. The power of the Shawanoes had been broken before he was born, in the early Indian wars, and he was determined to restore it. He conceived an even greater plan. The many Indian tribes had never been united; most often they had been at war with one another. Tecumseh proposed to unite them all, from the Great Lakes to Florida, in one warlike confederation whose purpose it should be to exterminate the white invaders and hold the country for the Indians alone.

Magnificent in stature, far famed as a hunter, a persuasive orator, Tecumseh had moved secretly toward the accomplishment of this vast plan. When Crockett and his family found a home near the Tennessee border he had already visited many tribes far to the north. Now he was traveling in the Mississippi Territory, through what became Alabama, with the purpose of arousing the Creeks. Runners had gone before him. When he marched into an open square of a large Creek village with a party of Ohio Indians he found the Creeks solemnly assembled there, naked except for gorgeous ornaments, their heads adorned with eagle plumes, their faces painted black. All had bound the emblem of the buffalo tail to their arms. Tecumseh broke into a harangue, and later in secret counsel with the chiefs transmitted his most urgent news.

The year was 1812, and the American war with the British had begun. Its thunder was now heard to the north, on the Great Lakes, in Canada, on the seas. Tecumseh told the Creeks of the British successes to the north and persuaded them that the outcome must be defeat for the Americans, declaring also that the British had promised him assistance in both the North and the South and that the Spanish would likewise join forces with the Indians.

A war party of Creeks was quickly formed, and the tribe became the most formidable of the American enemies in the South. Not all the Creeks were enlisted in this new war, however, for many had become friendly to the Americans and remained so at the risk of death from their own people. The Cherokees, now settled in the South, also tended toward peace and friendship.

Tecumseh did not live to see the outcome of his great scheme; he was killed in a preliminary battle. But he had enlisted the loyalty of another powerful figure, Weathersford, a half breed of fine presence and commanding power who lived with the Creeks and had great influence among them. Several months later, with Weathersford as leader, the Creeks attacked Fort Mimms in southern Alabama. A whole settlement of white men, women, and children was mercilessly put to death. A wounded Negro woman managed to escape. Finding a canoe on Lake Tensaw, she paddled fifteen miles to another fort bearing word of the mas-sacre.

Like other news this dire story traveled swiftly, softly through the western country. Within a short time in small scattered settlements volunteers were being raised for war against the Creeks.

"I've often thought about war, and I've heard people tell about it," said Crockett, "yet I never thought I could fight that way. But now I hear the wicked mischief done at the fort I know I must go."

Polly Crockett was still hardly more than a girl. Terrified, she begged Davy not to join the volunteers.

"But the next thing the Indians will be all about, bent on murder if we don't put a stop to it," he answered. "It'll only be for sixty days and anyway I must go. I believe I'm as able to go as any man in the country."

Polly cried a little, then turned about to her work. The autumn had begun, the harvest was in. She had often stayed alone in the cabin with the two boys when Crockett was hunting.

When the muster was called at Winchester some miles away Crockett was the second or third man who stepped out. A company of mounted riflemen was soon formed. Like Crockett, most of the volunteers had come riding their own horses, armed with their own rifles, in coonskin or foxskin caps, hunting shirts, deerskin leggings, and the moccasins they wore for hunting. "I believe this whole army is of the great grit," said Crockett.

In later years he wrote an account of his experiences in

the Creek War; it was a modest story as he told it. When a company of hunters was gathered together Crockett could match tall tales and tall talk with any man; but no one would guess from his own narrative that he was in the midst of nearly every important movement in this war and that he was chosen for scouting because of his skill with the rifle and his knowledge of wild land.

When all had been mustered in the mounted volunteers from Tennessee numbered about thirteen hundred, and these forces were the first to move against the Creeks. They were under the command of Colonel Coffee, one of the tall men of the West, quiet and unassuming, who fulfilled his duties and let anyone who wanted it have the glory of the outcome. General Andrew Jackson was in command of the entire army, including foot volunteers and militia. He had been hindered by official delays in moving south. The volunteers, in advance, rode into Alabama and crossed the Tennessee, camping on a high bluff overlooking the river.

Scouts were needed to go at once into the Creek country and discover the movements of the Indians. Crockett was chosen with twelve others for this dangerous and difficult enterprise.

The party crossed the Tennessee and found themselves among a settlement of Cherokees. Here they divided, with Crockett as leader of a band of five. He found a Cherokee who was willing to join him as a guide, but the Indian preferred not to march with the others by daylight. He promised to meet Crockett at a fork in a trace farther on after dark. When he drew near he was to hoot like an owl. "Then

I'll holler like an owl and you answer back the same way," said Crockett.

Dark came. No owl was heard. Crockett decided to leave the trace since this might be traveled by Creek runners, who in turn were thought to be seeking out the positions of the Americans. With his four companions he turned into the head of a hollow and struck camp. As he was beginning to wonder whether the Cherokee had betrayed him he heard a hoot. "My owl," he whispered, and gave the soft, wild, shrill notes in reply. Guided by the sound, the Cherokee reached the camp, and a route for the next day was quickly planned.

Following along Indian traces that none but an Indian or a skilled hunter like Crockett could see, the small party moved on south, traveling through a Cherokee town, then passing the cabin of a white man who had married a Creek woman. He told Crockett that ten painted Creek warriors had slipped by only an hour before. The man was surly and urged Crockett to leave. "If you're caught here we'll all be killed," he muttered.

At this point two or three of the volunteers wished to turn back, but Crockett refused. They pushed on toward a camp of Creeks, who were said to be friendly. From them Crockett hoped to learn of the movements of the war party. At nightfall Crockett and the others reached the camp and found there about forty men, women, and children. The men and boys had bows and arrows, and in the evening Crockett joined them in a shooting match by the flare of pine lights. The Indians enjoyed the match but they were clearly uneasy. They had little or nothing to say as to the movements of the hostile Creeks.

Crockett and his men tied their saddled horses near the place where they meant to sleep and lay down with their guns in their arms.

"I had just got into a doze when I heard the sharpest scream that ever came from the throat of a human creature," Crockett declared, telling the story. "It was more like a wrathy painter than anything else."

"Red Sticks," whispered one of his companions, and the five scouts were up and on their horses in an instant.

There was no attack. A Creek runner had screamed as he came into camp. He told Crockett that a great war party of more than a thousand Creeks had been crossing the Coosa River all day at the Ten Islands, to the southwest. This news greatly alarmed the Indians in camp, and they were up and away in a few minutes.

Crockett and his men also left quickly, riding hard to cover the sixty-five miles back to the volunteers' camp. They passed the Cherokee town they had seen the day before and found large fires were burning there, but the village was empty. Here the Cherokee guide left them, disappearing in shadow.

The little group of scouts skirted the blaze of the fires, preferring the dim and broken light of the moon and the darkness of the trees. They rode all night; at dawn they were still riding. At ten in the morning Crockett reported to Colonel Coffee. Soon afterward the other party of scouts rode in with similar news about the Creek war party.

THE INDIAN FIGHTER

Breastworks were thrown up around the camp, and a courier was sent in haste to General Jackson, who had now gathered the militia and foot volunteers about thirty miles away near the southern border of Tennessee. Jackson's order to his troops was given instantly. He brought his forces on a fast march to the new camp within five hours. His entire army was now assembled.

A new enemy appeared at once—hunger. An army of twenty-five hundred men required several hundred bushels of grain, tons of meat, gallons of whiskey, and many other stores each week. But provisions were arriving only in small quantities at irregular intervals. Food that was to come by the rivers was halted because the waters were low in autumn. There were long delays in the transmission of orders from Washington. Coffee's army had already foraged the country round about before Jackson arrived, so little remained in the way of food there.

Jackson watched the river like a hawk, hoping for arrival of supplies. His tall figure with the long lean yellow face could be seen striding up and down the great bluff as though he would wear the ground away by his impatience. He was sick, short tempered, and suffering from a wound in one shoulder which he had received some time before in a duel. He wrote furious letters to the authorities and to his friends. He also began to drill his hungry army.

It was at this time that Crockett became widely known among the volunteers from Tennessee. Beside the fires at night he would keep a whole large company in high spirits by his tales and his talk, poured from a memory that was long and clear. He told of his adventures over the eastern mountains as a boy and pictured the odd people who had stayed at his father's tavern. He mimicked the old German of the Shenandoah Valley, and some of the wagoners he had known, and the riverboatmen. He told of his adventures in hunting and repeated hunting stories he had heard from others. "I never would have believed I could remember so much!" he declared. When he lacked an old story he could always invent a strange or comical new one.

Throughout the army Crockett was soon known as the best fellow in the world, and as a man willing to share anything he had. "Crockett! Know that man Crockett?" His name echoed about the camp. Many years afterward his fellow soldiers talked of him with friendship.

At last Jackson brought the period of drill to an end. Still short of provisions, he decided to send out a contingent of mounted riflemen to scour for warring Creeks under Coffee. They could shift for themselves for food, and Jackson hoped that they could also discover and destroy some of the smaller Creek strongholds. The plan was for these men to make a wide circle and meet the main army a little farther to the south near the Ten Islands of the Coosa, where the Creek war party was supposed to be gathered. Crockett was chosen as a scout to accompany Coffee's contingent.

They crossed the Tennessee again since travel was better on the farther side, and followed its course back a little northwest to Muscle Shoals, where the river was shallow with a rough bottom. Here they forded, then pushed on south into the region of the Black Warrior River where hostile Creeks were known to dwell. After a day's ride they reached a Creek village that had recently been deserted. Fires were still burning in the town. A good supply of dried corn and a quantity of dried beans were found in the cribs. These were taken and the village burned.

On the move again, Crockett gained permission from Colonel Coffee to hunt as they traveled since no one had had meat for several days. He had gone only a short distance in the woods when he found a fine deer that had just been killed lying on the ground. By small signs he knew that this belonged to an Indian hunter. "I never was in favor of one hunter stealing from another," Crockett told his messmates, "but meat's so scarce I knew I was in for it."

Traveling toward the Coosa, the contingent came to the house of the surly white man, married to a Creek woman, whom Crockett had talked with on his scouting expedition. The house was empty, but from a Cherokee he learned a story which he reported to Colonel Coffee. The news of the Creek war party had been false.

"That white rascal sent the Indian runner at night to the camp, and had him let loose a cry like a savage painter, and then had him tell us that the Creeks had been crossing the Coosa all day at the Ten Islands. Nary a Creek there, says this Cherokee. It was all a false alarm, intended to deceive. We were mistaken, and I don't mind admitting it." The Creeks had succeeded in deceiving the other party of scouts as well.

The Americans, still with insufficient food, were adrift in a strange and hostile country, seeking a subtle enemy whom they could not find, who might spring upon them in overwhelming numbers from an unexpected quarter at any moment. This was to be their predicament throughout the war. But if Crockett and the other scouts were misled at times, it was they who were to discover the movements of the Creeks at important points and prepare the way for battle.

Coffee's contingent circled farther across country and met the main army. All then pushed on to the Ten Islands of the Coosa, where ten small green islands lay scattered in a wide river full of shoals. Truly enough, no Creeks were found there. A fort was soon established, and Crockett was sent out with a few others to spy the land. Slipping through underbrush and covering their tracks for fear they were being spied upon in turn, the little party succeeded in approaching the Creek town of Tallushatches about ten miles away. Returning, they described the safest ways of attack for the army.

Those hunters and settlers of the deep wilderness in southern Tennessee who had joined as volunteers under Coffee must have seemed to General Jackson among the bravest of his forces, for he sent them to take Tallushatches. Crockett was again among their number.

As the contingent was about to leave, a party of friendly Creeks came up, wearing white deer's tails and white feathers and begged to join them. Moving quietly, forming two semi-circles about the town, the army of Indians and hunters pressed forward and attacked a little after sunrise. The drums of the enemy began to beat, savage yells arose. The action was fierce and swift. The town was burned, the women and children taken prisoners. Five Americans were killed. The contingent returned to the Coosa.

Then once more the other enemy, hunger, appeared. The army at the Ten Islands had been on half rations ever since its arrival. Now even these were diminished. Some men, almost starving, began eating beef hides. And in spite of hunger the scouts were again in the thick of active trouble.

A runner came to Jackson's tent with a message from Fort Taledega, farther south, where about two hundred friendly Indians were assembled. Eleven hundred painted Creeks on the warpath had gathered near the fort and had informed the Indians there that if they failed within three days to come out and join them against the Americans they would take the fort and spare no one.

Jackson was quick to act. Hungry as they were, his men were soon on the march. A small party of scouts hurried on to discover the approaches. Crockett was of this number and afterwards told the story of the attack.

"We shaped things so the army would divide as at Tallushatches, going to the right and left of the fort. Our lines marched on till they met in front and then closed in the rear, forming a big hollow square, and old Major Russel then went on with his company to start the battle. When they got near the fort the top of it was lined with friendly Indians, crying out as loud as they could roar, 'How-dy-do, brother, how-dy-do?' They kept this up till Major Russel had passed by the fort and was moving on. Now the Creeks had concealed themselves under the bank of a branch that ran partly round the fort in the manner of a half moon. Russel was going right into their circle, for he couldn't see them, while the Indians on top of the fort were trying every plan to show him his danger. But he couldn't understand them. At last two of them jumped from the fort and ran and took his horse by the bridle and told him there was a thousand Creeks lying under the bank. At about this moment the Creeks fired and came rushing forth like a cloud of Egyptian locusts, and screaming like all the young devils had been turned loose, with the old devil of all at their head. They were all painted as red as scarlet and were just as naked as they were born. Russel's company quit their horses and took to the fort, and their horses ran up to our line, which had then advanced in full view. The warriors came yelling on, meeting us. They fought with guns and also with their bows and arrows, and at last they broke through a part of our line which was made up of drafted men."

The Americans were rapid in pursuit, and nearly five hundred Creek warriors were slain. But a large number of the war party escaped.

Still no provisions arrived. The weather began to turn cold. The clothing of many of the men was nearly gone, and their horses had grown thin and poor. Like Crockett, most of the volunteers had enlisted for sixty days, and that time was long since past. A group of their officers waited

THE ACTION WAS FIERCE AND SWIFT

on General Jackson and begged permission for the men to return home for fresh horses and clothing so as to be better prepared for another campaign. Jackson was short. He refused.

Now these frontiersmen were unaccustomed to military law. They had no intention of deserting, but they decided to take a furlough in spite of General Jackson. They gave their word that they would return, and this seemed enough to them.

Crockett joined in the bold informal decision. He told of it casually. "We began to fix for a start," he said. "And the general went out and placed his cannon on a bridge we had to cross, and ordered out some drafted men to keep us back. But we got ready and moved on till we came near the bridge. We had our flints picked and our guns primed so that if fired on we might fight our way through. When we came still nearer the bridge we heard the guards cocking their guns, and we did the same. We marched boldly on, and not a gun was fired, nor a life lost. We got home pretty safely, and in a short time had procured fresh horses and a supply of clothing better suited for the season. Then we went back to the camp on the Tennessee, where some new forces were gathered. Here we had a message from General Jackson, demanding that on our return we should serve out *six months*. Some decided to go back home. I knew if I went back home I wouldn't rest, for I felt it my duty to be out. And somehow or other when I *was* out I was always delighted to be in the very thickest of the danger. So a few of us determined to push on and join the army."

Jackson had assembled his army near the Talapoosa River to provoke an attack from the Creeks who were known to be gathered there. With a small band of seasoned scouts Crockett was sent at once to help locate the enemy. As the scouts stealthily followed the margins of a stream their practiced eyes found plenty of small signs that Indians had recently passed, but throughout the whole of the day only these slight and secret signs were visible. At night they camped with guns in their arms and with guards posted close about them.

About two hours before dawn the gun of one of the guards was fired. All were up in an instant, throwing brushwood on low embers and slipping into the darkness, hoping the Indians would rush into the firelight for an attack. They did not, but began shooting into the trees where the scouts lay. Watching the flashes of the Indian guns, Crockett and the others returned the fire as best they could, but four scouts were killed and at daylight the Indians had vanished. Whether any of them had fallen no one knew, for it was their custom to carry away their dead if possible. The scouts buried their own dead and raised a great heap of logs over the space, burning these to ashes, to conceal their losses.

The following night a great thunderstorm broke, and the Indians favored such a time for fighting, yet they did not attack. Jackson believed he had guessed their plan. Above the ford of the Talapoosa where he planned to cross was a narrow gorge that seemed created for an ambush. He was sure that the Creeks were waiting to attack his forces there. He arranged to cross at a ford lower down. If the Creeks discovered the change, as with their subtle scouts and runners they might, they would try to attack from the rear. He therefore commanded certain forces to form a rear guard. The company of scouts to which Crockett belonged was among these forces.

Jackson's surmises were right. The Creeks discovered the new plan and as the rear of the army was crossing a stream that flowed into the Talapoosa nearly a thousand painted warriors bore down upon them, wildly whooping and yelling. A rain of bullets and a cloud of arrows descended as many of the men waded up to their waists or the horses' flanks. The militia, which had been ordered to form the main portion of the rear guard, broke and ran in a cowardly fashion with two colonels at their head. The artillery, now on the farther side of the stream, was quickly disabled by the Creeks, who picked off the gunners. Other artillerymen could not bring the single cannon into action because in the confusion the rammer had been broken and the picker lost.

With the company of scouts Crockett was midstream on horseback when the Creeks attacked. Wheeling in counterattack, the scouts turned and swept out of the water toward the Indians and by their swift action succeeded in dividing a band of the warriors. Forcing a large number into retreat they followed them hotly through a shower of arrows and bullets and succeeded in pushing them into the back country, pausing only when the last of the Indians had taken to the neighboring hills. In this daring headlong ride there had always been the chance of further ambush by smaller bands of Creeks; and with the militia in retreat the scouts had had no way of knowing whether they would be supported.

"When I saw those two colonels of the militia a running I was mad all over. I was burning inside like a tar kiln, and I wonder the smoke wasn't pouring out of me on all sides," said Crockett to one of the other scouts as they rode back to the river. "I suppose that's what they would call a *forced march*," he added scornfully.

Crockett gave credit for the bold ride of the scouts to Colonel Carroll, who had led the company. "Colonel Carroll showed greater bravery than any man I ever saw. If it hadn't been for Carroll we should all have been genteelly licked that time, for we were in a devil of a fix, part of our men on one side of the creek, part on the other, and the Indians all the time pouring in on us as hot as fresh mustard on a sore shin."

The quick action of the scouts had probably saved the army, even though Jackson himself had brought the cannon into action. In the midst of hot fire from the enemy he had ridden to the small group of artillerymen and pulled the ramrod out of his own musket to use as a rammer. One of the men quickly converted a bayonet into a picker, and the cannon was used with disastrous effect upon the remaining Creeks.

Jackson in his dry, terse manner praised the small company of scouts to which Crockett belonged. "They realized and even exceeded my expectations," he said briefly. "I could always have sure reliance on those men."

The next movements of Crockett make a small riddle. His horse had been crippled by this last hard ride against the Creeks, but the wish to save a valued animal can hardly account for his journey to Tennessee after this battle. The six months of service which Jackson had demanded had not yet passed, nor even the sixty days which Crockett and some others had promised. Sharp, imperious, often apparently aloof, Jackson understood men well, and Crockett was well known to others in command. He may have been sent on a mission of which he never felt at liberty to speak. With all his easy talk he could keep a secret better than most men. Even when he could score against someone whom he disliked he rarely related matters that closely concerned others. Years afterward in referring to the two colonels who had fled from action on the Talapoosa he refused to speak their names, saying, "Nothing could be gained by it."

Crockett always said that he went to Tennessee at this time because of his crippled horse; it may be that in the high-handed manner of the frontiersman he went home merely because he wished to. For a short time he visited Polly and his children. What else he did remains obscure. When he returned to Alabama the final battle with the Creeks had been fought at Horseshoe Bend, and Jackson was treating with the chiefs of the tribe.

6

BREEZES OF LUCK

A GREAT concourse of Creeks and Cherokees was as
sembled in that place near the Talapoosa called by the
Indians the Holy Ground. Jackson had shrewdly arranged
the gathering there, knowing that many Indians believed
that no white man could enter this place and that all would

incline to regard the proceedings there as sacred. A great glitter of bright beads, feathers, fine furs, showed among the members of the two tribes assembled outside Jackson's great marquee. Soldiers were drawn up in ranks. The two races studied each other unobtrusively across the silence. Within, the chiefs conferred through long hours with Jackson. A young man named George Mayfield, whom Crockett had known in eastern Tennessee, had been chosen to act as Jackson's interpreter because of his knowledge of the Creeks, their ways and their language.

George Mayfield had been stolen by the Creeks as a baby during one of their early raids. As the Indians came to know the powerful ways of the white man they wanted white children to live with their own children, thinking that the young Indians might learn the secret of that power. When Mayfield reached manhood he had been permitted to choose whether he would remain with the tribe or return to his own people, whose movements his Creek foster-parents had traced. He chose to return, and was sent back with a gift of fine horses and other handsome possessions, but he had never felt at ease among the whites. He had the silent ways of an Indian. Afterwards he lived for months at a time with the tribe among which he had grown up.

A bond existed between Crockett and Mayfield besides an acquaintance in that part of Tennessee where both were born. This was the subtle and many-sided attraction of Indian life. In crude forms many men of the frontier felt this, even when they roughly declared that they wanted to see the complete extermination of the tribes. White renegades had often fought with the Indians against the whites. In border warfare frontiersmen often fell into a frenzy, adopted Indian tactics, and scalped the enemy. In peaceful times white men had gone to dwell in Indian villages of their own accord. To see hunters on the frontier out for game was to notice how closely they resembled Indian hunters. They wore fringed deerskin, moccasins, and carried tomahawks; they quickly learned the habits of uncanny observation that belonged to the Indians and had an endurance similar to theirs.

Crockett's grandparents had been massacred by warring Creeks; his people had lived with a sharp consciousness of danger from this alien enemy through all his childhood. He had just been engaged in warfare against them. But friendly Creeks and Cherokees had joined with him then, and through the years his liking for the Indians had steadily grown. This was to become an allegiance of a rare order; and at the moment events were shaping that much later were to bring this allegiance into dramatic play. As Jackson imposed a treaty upon the Creeks he made decisions and perhaps then reached fixed conclusions which were to become highly fateful. At this time a final turn was given to the destiny of all the five tribes of the Southwest.

Within the marquee the proceedings were slow, for the Indians would consider no matter of importance without ceremonials. Big Warrior, colossal, renowned for his oratory, never hostile to the whites, was there with other celebrated chiefs. They wore ceremonial ornaments and dress; they made ceremonial gifts; they made speeches.

They listened to the terms which Jackson had to offer. Half the ancient Creek domain was demanded by Jackson for the United States government.

Talk through the interpreter went on. Big Warrior said —as was true—that many Creeks and Cherokees had fought with the whites against their own people in the recent war, and that he himself had done so, that the treaty made by the Creeks long ago with Father Washington might not be broken. "To his friendly arm I hold fast. I will never break the chain of friendship we made together. He was father to the Muscoga people, and not only to them but to all the people under the sun! His talk I now hold in my hand." Big Warrior held out the treaty bearing Washington's signature. He then told the story of the recent war, and admitted that the American claim for indemnity was just. He said that the friendly Creeks were willing to give up part of their land, but he insisted that the habits of the Indians were not always the habits of white men. They required large hunting grounds. To surrender half of their domain would bring them to great distress.

Shelokta spoke, a friendly chief who had fought under Jackson's command throughout the war. He begged Jackson to leave the Creeks in possession of the rich country west of the Coosa.

The talk quietly, politely droned on. At last the conference was ended, the treaty signed. The Creeks had yielded to the demands of the government. At the same time the United States, through Jackson, guaranteed to the Creek nation their right to own "forever" the land that remained to them. But this promise was not kept; and the cession of territory by the Creeks to the United States was the beginning of a procedure by which all of the five tribes —the Creeks, the Cherokees, the Chickasaws, the Choctaws, the Seminoles—were removed from their lands, though they were peaceable.

At the time—indeed for long afterward—Crockett can have had no notion that he was to have a share in events that followed these momentous proceedings. He was a frontiersman, one of many—unlettered, unprosperous, careless of the future. But in later years he was to come into collision with Jackson himself over the issue of the right of the Indians to retain the lands ceded to them.

When the treaty was concluded he joined a contingent of Jackson's army that scouted against small bands of hostile Creeks who still roved through the South. He went southwest as far as Fort Mimms, and southeast to Pensacola. Again these soldiers went hungry, and Crockett was greatly occupied with the precarious business of hunting in a country already ravaged. Occasionally he found "a fine chance of honey." Once he traded powder and shot with a settler for parched corn. There were many skirmishes with parties of Creeks.

At last the whole thundering War of 1812 was over, Jackson's triumph at New Orleans was complete. Crockett received an honorable discharge from the army; he rejoiced when the war was over. "I never liked this business with the Indians," he said. "I'm glad I'm through with these war matters. They have no fun in them at all. It was nothing but dog eat dog."

Crockett had a short period of happiness with Polly and his children. The boys, John and William, had grown fast, and a little girl was born, whom he called Polly. Hunting was plentiful, and he accumulated fine furs. But within a few months Polly sickened and died. This was a great blow to Crockett, for he had loved her; he never forgot her. Over her grave in the forest he placed huge limestone bowlders like a cairn. He found he could no longer remain in the cabin by the deep stream.

Restlessly with his small children he moved again into wild country, this time some eighty miles farther west in Tennessee, to new land on Shoal Creek. Here he met Elizabeth Patton, whose husband had been killed in the Creek War; Crockett had known him. Elizabeth also had young children, a boy and a girl. "We're both in the same situation," Crockett said to her. "It might be we could do something for each other." They were married, and lived in comfort together. Crockett always spoke of the whole Patton connection as if it were his own.

Before long he had decided on a new move. "I'm going to see new country, something wilder than hereabouts," he said to Elizabeth, "and we might go there when I've looked it over."

In the autumn he was off to the southwest, traveling into the land of the Creeks and the Choctaws. He started with two or three others but was soon separated from them.

The journey was unlucky. One night he hobbled his

horse and lay down to rest. He was awakened by the sound
of the horse's bells, and these quickly grew faint. He followed the bells all night and walked all the next day, sometimes hearing them, sometimes losing them. At last he decided to turn back and continue his journey on foot. After
walking for several days to the south he fell sick. Some
Indians came up to him as he lay under a tree and offered
him melons, but he could not eat them. They made signs
to show him that he would die and be buried in the ground;
then they bore him to a nearby cabin, where he was cared
for. After a time he seemed well enough to travel and he
turned toward home, but again on the way he fell ill and
found refuge among strange people. He lay near death
for many weeks.

At last when early spring came and wild geese were honking overhead on their long flight north Crockett was able
to leave, though he was thin, pale, and very weak. A
wagoner carried him to a point within twenty miles of his
cabin and he walked the rest of the distance. Elizabeth had
believed he was dead. The runaway horse had made his
way home. Men had told her of talking with others in the
South who said they had seen Crockett die and had helped
bury him. "I knowed that was a whopper of a lie the minute I heard it!" said Crockett.

He now owned several good horses and had more household gear than when he had traveled over the Cumberlands a few years before. Instead of a pair of dogs a restless
pack now snuffed at his heels. Again he hunted, but he was
soon entangled by other matters.

The new land was so wild that no government had been set up there. Dangerous characters roamed freely through the country, and a regiment of militia had been organized by settlers scattered at far distances for many miles around. Crockett was elected colonel of this regiment.

It seemed that he was never to be clear of a hotchpotch of people, for not many months later he was elected magistrate as well.

"This will be hard business for me," he told those who urged him to take the office. "I can just barely write my name." He finally gave his consent. "That man's judgments stick like a wax plaster," said an admiring settler.

Finding that he would be obliged not only to write his name but make out warrants and keep a record of his proceedings, Crockett began to read whatever he could find and to practice the art of handwriting. This was slow work, but he made progress. It was at this time that he began to inscribe a motto at the end of documents. "Be always sure you're right, then go ahead."

Once more his fame grew in spite of him. He hunted widely as before, and again stories were told of his skill in the far backwoods. "Why, that man Crockett don't even need to shoot game if he don't care to!" said a neighbor. "Out in the woods one day he looked up into the top of a tall sycamore and there was a coon. He looked at the coon and the coon looked at him. And the coon piped up, 'Don't shoot, Colonel, I'll come down!' Even the varmints of the forest knows him."

When in 1821 the time came to elect a member for the

state legislature Crockett's name was mentioned. He cared nothing for the office and went off to North Carolina with a drove of cattle to sell there, traveling through the country he had known as a runaway boy. When he returned three months later electioneering was in full swing all over the large scantily settled district, and there were several candidates in the field. He was urged to enter the contest in earnest.

"The thought of making a speech makes my knees feel mighty weak," he confided to Elizabeth. "You could as well go to a pigsty for wool as to look to me for a speech. But I might just try it."

When he went out to a gathering of people Crockett had what he called "a breeze of luck." Men had come from miles around, starting out at dawn and arriving early. "As soon as they come the other candidates got at it, and they spoke most all day, and when they quit everybody was wore out!" said Crockett. "So I got up and told a story or two, and then I let 'em go. Afterwards they all pushed up for a horn, and I talked here and there amongst them. There was nothing more to it. That's what I call a breeze of luck—for the others to wear out the people first."

The next day another gathering was held at a distant point and Crockett was induced to show himself there. A barbecue was to wind up the day with a squirrel hunt beforehand. Crockett led a party of the squirrel hunters, and his party came off first. Then while blue smoke curled from the barbecue, and bear meat and venison were roasting, he talked and told stories.

Perhaps the people of the district liked him for his good nature and his story telling, and because he seemed to care very little whether he gained office or not. He admitted afterward that he didn't know at the time what "the judiciary" was. But he moved easily among other settlers like himself, in hunter's garb, a fine figure of a man, now more than six feet tall, broad shouldered, still young, with high color, his black hair worn long like that of most hunters.

Crockett was elected, but if a breeze of luck had come his way it was a light one. While he was away for a meeting of the legislature a disaster occurred through which he lost nearly everything he had. He had built a grist mill, a powder mill, and distillery, all connected, on a stream that ran through his land. He had been obliged to borrow a considerable sum to complete the buildings. With the spring rains a great freshet arose and carried them away.

When Crockett returned and saw the torn empty space where they had stood Elizabeth spoke to him quickly, 'Pay up, Davy. We'll sell everything to pay our debts and then move on. We'll scuffle for more."

"This is just the kind of talk I want to hear," Crockett answered. "A man's wife can make him pretty uneasy if she begins to scold and fret and perplex him when he has a full wagon load on his mind already. I'm glad you don't advise me to smuggle up this, that, and t'other so as to go on easy. We'll take a bran-fire new start. Stand up to the rack, fodder or no fodder! Anyway this part of the land is getting too much filled up."

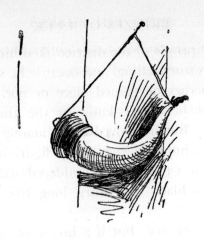

7

INTO THE SHAKES

IN THE year 1811 befell one of the great earthquakes in the known history of the world, in western Tennessee near the Mississippi River. Age-old trees were twisted from top to root. Deep cracks opened in the earth and fissures split the river bends. The river became a booming flood whose huge waves pushed far inland to overflow in small streams. The first steamboat to navigate the Mississippi, the *New Orleans,* commanded by Nicholas Roosevelt, approached this stretch of territory just before the great upheaval. The pilot saw that a storm was approaching and made fast to the riverbank for the night. Before long the great shivering motion began. The riverbank became an island. At dawn the island began to sink and finally disappeared. Through the skill of the pilot the steamer escaped into less turbulent waters though no landmarks now existed; but flatboats were caught in the vortex, lifted high in the air, and sunk. With a whirl of furious movement the river turned about on its current and flowed upstream for a time. It was only because there was as yet little river travel, because the land there was but sparsely inhabited that a great human devastation was not wrought.

The country came to be known as the Shakes. Father Marquette had passed its margin nearly a hundred and fifty years before in his canoe and had been welcomed some miles below by Indians. For many decades the Chickasaws had dwelt there undisturbed. Like the Cherokees, they had at last been persuaded to cede their land to the United States, but they still hunted there since few white men had cared to penetrate this strange and tangled land. This was now full of turbulent small rivers and wide lakes.

Among these was a short deep river that emptied into the Mississippi. According to a Chickasaw legend an Indian chief had lived by its banks before the earthquake, whose only son was born with a club foot that made him reel as he walked. Though his father tried to please and arouse him he was always an unhappy lad. When he grew to manhood he wandered to the south among the Choctaws, where he saw a most beautiful Indian maiden whom he loved at once and wished to marry. Her father refused to give his daughter to a man with a club foot. When Reelfoot succeeded in stealing the maiden the Choctaw chief put a curse upon him and all his tribe, saying that the Great Spirit would stamp upon their land in anger and destroy it.

When the earthquake came this was taken by the Indians to be the outcome of the curse and the prophecy. The mouth of the river was dammed by the upheaval and a long deep winding lake was created, which was called the Reelfoot. It was wild and strange, with cypresses showing their black-green tops in lines above the water. The earthquake had shaken them many feet below the hillsides where they had grown. Soon the lake was covered by great yellow lilies, so that to come upon it suddenly was to find a yellow light glowing in the midst of the shadowed water. Mink, otter, beaver were to be found there. Wild geese haunted the shore. Here too were the great snapping turtles with great heads and armored scales that became famous in Tennessee legend. It was to one of these that a hunter had referred when he said that Davy was cradled in a snapping turtle's shell.

Other smaller lakes had been sunk within the land. The Obion River was a short distance south of the Reelfoot, then the Forked Deer, and the Hatchie, all flowing westward into what the Indians called the Old Big Deep Strong River.

For nearly a year deep quakes continued, stirring the region across the river as well. At their heaviest they were noticed by the Indians in Canada; they were felt in New Orleans, and eastward as far as Boston. For some time light quakes were often felt. When Crockett came into this region in 1822 to take up land and build a cabin his cap was shaken from his head as he was planting corn.

The land was immensely fertile, so fertile that the settler was hindered rather than helped by the rich soil. Great trees still remained, and others quickly sprang up—gum, walnut, pecan, sassafras, hickory, and the delicious white plum that had been offered Father Marquette. There were deep tangles of large sweet wild grapes. Here and there canebrakes made a labyrinthine wilderness, with paths trodden by wild creatures on their way to a stream or to the salt licks. The cane grew from twelve to thirty feet in height, on the richest soil, often beneath great trees and along the rivers. Hunters were obliged to cut their way through the dense thickets with their knives or to wedge their way backward through them. Soon after the great earthquake a hurricane had passed over this region, leveling many trees, stacking the cane in dense masses. Perhaps because of this, perhaps because of the crowding, slapping cane and the perils that lurked there, western settlers called a canebrake "a harricane." Black bears and panthers haunted the brakes.

The land was hard to clear but everywhere there was a great abundance of game—black bear, deer, even elk, panthers, wildcats, coons, possums, squirrels, turkeys in great numbers. For many years this was almost lost territory, known only to a few trappers and hunters. In later times men called it the land of the Chickasaws and Davy Crockett.

Early in the spring of 1822 Crockett set out for this region with John, his oldest boy, on foot. Provisions were packed on one of the horses, and two hunting dogs followed, old Whirlwind and Soundwell. It was a long rough journey. They were obliged to ford the Tennessee at high water where it turned north toward the Ohio. When they reached the Shakes, Crockett chose a tract of land near the Obion a few miles south of Reelfoot Lake. The first settler had come into this country only three years before, and the nearest cabin was seven miles away. There was none other for more than fifteen miles.

Hobbling the horse, Crockett and his son set out to explore the country across the Obion. The river had overflowed its banks and stretched like a wide lake as far as eye could see. They took to the water, sometimes walking on the bottom, swimming when they had to. Far on the other side was a flatboat, bound up the river with provisions. They made for it, and the boatmen gave them shelter for the night.

Elizabeth heard the story later.

"The next day it rained riproariously," Crockett said "and the river rose considerably, but not enough for the boat to move upstream. So I got the boatmen to go over with me to where I was going to settle, and we slapped up a cabin in little or no time. I bought four barrels of meal some salt, and a big middling of bacon from the boatmen and left all in the cabin. For pay I agreed to help move the boat. We got up the river very well, but quite slowly and we landed on the eleventh day at the place where the load was to be delivered.

"Then I got a skiff and we cut down the river for the

cabin. A young man came with me, and we turned in and planted corn. The place has a little open prairie. It was so late I didn't make rails to fence it, but there's nothing to disturb our corn except the wild varmints, and the old serpent himself couldn't keep 'em out with a fence to help him if they want to get in. The cabin is set near a living spring.

"It's all a wilderness," Davy added with satisfaction, "and the woods was full of Indians, hunting. We'll get together our little plunder and go."

The family procession set out, a lively party. There were now eight children in all, the two youngest so small that Crockett carried them much of the way perched on his shoulders or asleep in his arms while the older boys led the horses. No one rode, not even Elizabeth.

Deer, possums, and coons had spared the corn in the new clearing, and the Crocketts were soon settled. Besides corn there was another crop, for Davy had sowed a few gourd seeds, and the long sprawling vines with their great yellow bottles lay far over the little prairie. Dry gourds could be used for dippers or as milkpans when milk was to be had, or to keep sugar in, or wild honey. Negroes in the back country made fiddles out of gourds.

As soon as the crop was in Davy began to hunt. The wild face of the country lay before him, and he had much to do before winter began—furs to seek, bear meat and venison to find, and small game. Bear and deer he found at once. Often he took the boys hunting with him, teaching them to discover deer against the brown bushes and to lie quiet and disguise themselves when they heard a rustle or saw the flicker of a white tail. If a deer was grazing nearby Crockett could turn himself into something that appeared to be a gnarled stump, with his fur cap like old tufted moss, his head bent, his hands hidden. When he wanted to find a clear space for aim he sometimes got down on all fours, snorting and rooting along toward the deer like a wild hog. Curled and humped in the grass his smallest boys looked like big jack rabbits in their fur coats and caps as they watched him.

With the boys Crockett went to a small sunken lake where a water line ran along the trunks of the bordering trees, high up, marking the place where water rose in the spring. Even in autumn many trees were set deep in the water. Black oaks, the graceful pecan, the delicate spreading beech—bronze and red and purple—lifted their tops above the silvery surface and were mirrored there. Squirrels lived in the treetops nearest the shore. A hunter in a canoe could have looked into their nests. In the thickets nearby were raccoons, possums, deer. Crockett and his boys came home laden with game.

"See that little dark hummock of weed over there amongst the beech leaves," said William to Robbie, the smallest boy, as they tramped toward the cabin at dusk. "That's a possum and no mistake. If you was to go up to him he'd be stiff as a poker with that grin on his little face."

Some Chickasaws passed in the shadow. "Good hunting neighbors," said Crockett.

At night every cranny of the cabin would be lighted by

a great hickory fire. Elizabeth would be spinning, and young Polly would wind the ball. One of the heavy packs brought by the Crocketts into the Shakes was filled with flax and wool. There were always stories—stories of wild beasts and their ways, among others. It would have been strange if settlers friendly to the Indians, like Crockett, had not picked up some of their many tales about animals. He came to know the Chickasaws and Choctaws well, living in the Shakes. One way or another he had known many Cherokees, in Tennessee and in the Mississippi Territory —known them under friendly circumstances. His own tales often had a touch of animal impersonation. Consider him then, cleaning and oiling his rifle—"my Betsey"—and asking his boys if they ever heard why a possum's tail is bare.

"Seems the possum used to have a long bushy tail same as the coon's or even handsomer, and he was so proud of it that he used to comb it out every morning and every night, and he made a song about it that he used to sing at the frolics. The rabbit was jealous, for you could hardly notice *his* tail at all. So the rabbit made up his mind to play the possum a trick. There was to be a big frolic and all the animals in the woods was going.

"It was the rabbit's business to send out the news, so as he was passing the possum's house he stopped and asked him if he was coming to the frolic. 'I'll come,' said the possum, 'if I can have a special seat. I have such a handsome tail that I ought to sit where everybody can see it.' And he spoke rather short and nippy. The rabbit said yes, the possum could have a special seat, and he promised to send someone to comb and dress the possum's tail to make it look extra nice.

"Then the rabbit went over to see the cricket, and he told him just what to do. When the morning of the frolic came the cricket went to the possum's house, and the possum stretched himself out and shut his eyes and took his ease, while the cricket went about his work. He combed that tail and he combed it with those little forelegs of his, with little fine teeth in 'em like in a comb. And he wrapped a red string around the possum's tail to keep it smooth till night for the frolic. But all the time he was a winding that red string he was a clipping and a cutting off all the hair. You know a cricket can cut most anything with his little sharp scissors, even a web of cloth.

"The possum kept the red string on all day and he had it on at night when he went to the frolic. The best seat was ready for him, the way the rabbit promised. The drummers began to drum, and the fiddlers began to fiddle, and all the animals began to stamp their feet. Then the possum loosened the red string and skipped out into the middle of the floor and began a singing his song. 'See my beautiful tail!' he sang. Everybody shouted, and he danced around in a circle, and sang, 'See what a beautiful color it is!' They shouted again, and he danced around and sang, 'See how it sweeps the ground!' Then he sang, 'See how fine the fur is!'

"Then all the animals laughed, and they laughed so long the possum wondered what they were laughing at. He looked around and pretty soon he looked down at his tail, and it was bare as a lizard's tail. He was mighty astonished and ashamed. He couldn't say a word. He just rolled over onto the ground the way a possum will do when he's surprised. And he just stayed there and grinned."

There was a laugh and a pause. Since it was the custom among hunters to match one story with another William spoke up. "An Indian boy told me a different story. He said the old possum lost his tail because he wanted rings round it like a coon's. Somebody made out to him he could singe 'em on with fire, and he burned all the fur off his tail and most burned himself to a cracklin' besides."

"I heard how he got his grin," said Robbie. "The old possum was hungry when he was walking through the woods, and he saw a nice sweet little plum on the ground. Anyway he thought it was a plum. But it was a bitter oak ball that puckered his mouth up and made him grin and he's been a grinnin' ever since."

Just then there was a faint tremor that set the furs hanging from the rafters swinging. "I s'pose that's our old earthquake," said Robbie.

"This cabin's a sitting on the earthquake's grave," said William.

They looked outside, but the earth was still except for the snap of a twig and the creak of frost.

When Christmas drew near wild meat hung in the cabin and beside the doors. Some Chickasaws, passing by on their winter hunt, had left a gift of rabbits and turkey gobblers. Tall and stately, they had paused for only a few moments at this new cabin of the white man. The gift was welcome for Crockett was out of powder. "This meat won't last long with ten in the family," he said to Elizabeth, "and anyway we have to have powder to shoot off for Christmas. I know there's been another of Noah's floods, but I must have my powder."

A friend had settled in the autumn across the Obion near one of its forks and had brought a keg of powder for Crockett on the journey into the Shakes. Crockett had been too busy hunting to go after it and now the Obion had overflowed its banks after the rains.

Elizabeth opposed the trip. "The river's a mile wide anyway from hill to hill, and we might as well all starve as for you to freeze to death or get drowned."

But Crockett tied up some dry clothing and moccasins in a bundle, took his gun and hunting tools, and started. The snow was about four inches deep; the weather had turned cold. He admitted afterward that when he reached the river it looked like an ocean, stretching wide and gray. He had no canoe. He stepped into the water and waded along the flooded ground until he came to the channel. Here was a long log above water. He mounted the log, and balancing with his gun and bundle, he crossed the channel. Then he waded again over flooded ground until he reached a deep slough that he knew well. He had often crossed the slough to a small island raised part way across, using a sunken log as a bridge.

The log, if there, lay three or four feet beneath the surface, and below it was a further depth of eight or ten feet of water. He felt for the log cautiously with his feet, but could not find it. He could swim, but he had to keep his gun and bundle dry.

In times of low water a tall stout sapling stood alongside the log. The sapling was still there, a dozen feet away from where he stood. At his side were other saplings, a clump of them. Laying his gun in the crotch of one and tying his bundle to a branch, he cut another below the crotch. This he lodged against the sapling in the slough, thrusting it firmly within some branches. The end nearest him he fastened in the crotch of another tree.

Then he cut a pole and crawled along his bridge until he reached the sapling in the slough. Here with his pole he felt for the log, and found it. It was as deep as he supposed, and seemed firm, making a bridge to the farther side of the slough, but he dared not risk traveling back along it for his gun and bundle. Slowly he returned along the sapling bridge, took the gun and bundle, crept back again, and finally let himself down upon the sunken log. He felt his way along this with his feet, balancing, in water about waist deep. "It was ticklish business," he admitted afterward.

The log held firm as he traversed the end of it. He came to a stretch of flooded ground, crossed it, and came to another slough over which a long log had been placed as a bridge. This was now loosened and was floating in the water. Crockett mounted the log, thinking that with care he could walk along it but when he had reached the middle of deep water the log rolled over and he went down, quickly thrusting his gun and bundle above his head as he went. The water came up to his neck. Keeping his gun and bundle in the air he walked slowly along the bottom until he reached another wide space of flooded ground where the water was shallow again.

When at last he waded ashore his feet were numb. He had been in icy water all the way except when he was crossing the high log and when he was crawling back and forth on his sapling bridge. But his gun and his bundle were dry. He changed his clothes and tried to run so as to warm himself a little, but he could only trot. At last he covered the five miles to his friend's cabin. The family could hardly believe that he had crossed the river at such a time.

The next morning was piercing cold, and Crockett was persuaded not to start for home that day. He went hunting instead and brought in two deer. The weather grew colder, and his friend insisted that he would be unable to return home for some time. But Crockett knew that his wife and children would soon be without food, and he set out.

When he reached the river with his keg of powder, his gun, and bundle a sheet of ice lay before him as far as he could see. He hadn't gone far over it before the ice broke. Shifting his load to one arm, he took out his tomahawk and opened the way before him until he found a place where the ice was thick enough to bear his weight. But it broke again, and he was obliged to wade until he came to the floating log that had rolled him into the water. This was now frozen fast in the ice. He crossed on it without much difficulty and worked along until he reached the log under water in the slough.

The swiftness of the current here had kept the water

from freezing. Crockett found the log and managed to balance his load and keep a foothold, moving slowly until he reached his sapling bridge. Then he had to make two trips back and forth, one for the keg of powder, one for his gun and bundle. At last through broken ice and water he reached the high log set on the other side. As he crept over the last stretch of ice toward high ground he came to an open broken trail. He decided a bear had gone that way and he decided to follow the bear, but the trail led to his cabin, and he found it had been made by a young man, traveling past, who had volunteered to go out and look for him.

Elizabeth and the children thought he had been lost in the icy current. "No, I'm not dead," said Crockett, "but there was times when I felt mighty nigh it. I've got my powder, and that's what I went for, and it's dry too."

The next morning he was out at sunrise with the two older boys. They hunted hard most of the day, finding small game in abundance but nothing more. Toward midafternoon William came galloping through the woods with word that he had seen two elk. He showed the direction they had taken. Crockett had only four balls left, and the boys had none. "I think I'll go after the elk," he said, "and I reckon I'd better go alone." The boys started homeward with the load of small game.

The afternoon was calm and still and frosty. Crockett walked for some distance through the woods, seeing only squirrels, or an occasional raccoon or possum. He did not fire, wishing to save powder and bullets, fearing also that gun-fire might alarm the elk. He walked until the sun was hardly more than two hours high, and at last he found what he was looking for. The ground was hard. The elk had left no tracks, but Crockett noticed places where the grass was bruised a little and saw a few bushes where either elk or deer had nibbled. As the nibbled leaves were very high he decided that he had found the trail of the elk. After another mile he saw two elk feeding in an open space. He approached so quietly that they did not hear him.

Since there were no trees nearby he got down and rooted his way toward them like a wild hog, but they got wind of something, and turned their heads back and looked at him, then ran off a little way. Rooting along as they moved, he followed them into some woods. When the elk began to feed again he stood up behind a tree, then ran as hard and as lightly as he could to a nearer tree. He peeped out after a moment, saw them feeding, and ran still nearer. The woods were open. As Crockett made ready to fire, he heard a sudden rustle, and saw five deer coming toward him. He raised Betsey and dropped the largest, than a second one, then a third, for they hadn't moved.

"I never saw anything like it before in all my hunting," he said afterwards. "I don't believe they ever saw a man before, for they wasn't in the least afraid of me."

But the two elk had fled, crashing through the woods. With only one ball left Crockett decided that he still must have his elk, and following their traces he walked for more than an hour before he saw them again. At last he came upon the two great beasts feeding in an open space. They appeared restless and shy. He couldn't get a close shot. The sun was down, and it was dim. Dodging among the trees that thickly bordered the little prairie, he at last got one of the elk within range. Quickly, surely, he leveled and fired, and the great creature fell. The other ran among the dusky trees, then stopped and wheeled. Even when Crockett came forward into the clearing the elk did not run but began to paw the ground and shake his head with its great horns branching six feet high and wide across. He lowered them angrily, pawed the ground again, then with a great crash bounded forward. Crockett could not fire for his last shot was gone, nor would he run as the animal bore down upon him. He gave a sudden shrill high cry, and the elk wheeled and was lost in the woods.

He dragged the elk he had brought down to the place where the deer lay, left it, and took one of the deer across his shoulders and walked home through the dark, sure of the way for he had hunted through this country before. The next morning the boys helped him bring the other deer and the elk to the cabin.

"But I can't waste more time without hunting bears," said Crockett that night, "for bears is fat now, and they'll be going into their holes for winter soon. We must have enough bear meat to last a long while. Tomorrow I'll try the harricane."

In the night a heavy rain fell, turning to sleet before morning. When Crockett rose the bushes were white, bent, and locked together with ice. "The ground looks slippery as a soaped eel," he said, "but I'll go all the same."

Outside the cabin the dogs were snuffing and crying. "My dogs always know when there's going to be a bear hunt." As he went out they bounded up against him—Whirlwind, Old Rattler, Soundwell, Tiger, Growler, Holdfast, Grim, Deathmaul, and Thunderbolt. Years had passed since Crockett brought Whirlwind over the Cumberlands. This dog was too old to hunt now. Crockett took only five of the dogs, with Soundwell as lead, whose deep tones could be heard at far distances.

They were soon off, slipping and sliding over the ice. This was to be no hunt for boys, and Crockett went alone to the big "harricane." He promised to return at night with a bear but when night came he had not appeared. Nor did he come the next night. In the meantime a heavy snow had fallen.

Toward dusk of the third evening his tall figure was seen striding toward the cabin. He had a heavy pack on his shoulders, and his dogs were limping at his heels with heads down.

That night Crockett told his story. "It took us quite a while to get to the harricane because of the ice, but once there my dogs began prowling round, and soon they were up. I gave them the word, and they went off in full cry with Soundwell singing out like a bell and the others most as true. The bear was sliding along through the cane, and 'twas such a thick place I was afraid the dogs would lose him. It's a wonder to me they ever got through that part of the brake. I had to go myself for more than a mile after that bear on my hands and knees, creeping through briars.

WITH A GREAT CRASH THE ELK BOUNDED FORWARD

If I hadn't had on deer leather clothes the briars would have picked me to pieces.

"The first thing I knew I was up to my neck in a sink hole of water. It made me so mad I had a good notion not to get out of it but I began to think that wouldn't spite anybody so out I scrambled. I could hear the old bear a rustling through the canebrake beyond, and the canes crashing. I harked my dogs on and presently I could hear my dogs and the bear fighting. They sang out, but the bear got away in the tangle. On we went till we come to the big creek, and there was the bear swimming across. My dogs plunged in and made a streak across the water following that bear. It was now past noon, and they had been running since sunrise, and we had passed through the harricane, which of itself was a day's work.

"All at once I heard my dogs fighting on the other side. This put me all in a storming humor and I rolled an old log I saw at my feet into the creek, which is pretty wide just there. I straddled the log with my feet in the water, and pushed off, paddling with one hand and pushing with my feet and holding up my gun. The log was old and didn't half float, so I was up to my thighs, but I got over safe and pushed the log up the bank to go back on. Way off in the distance I heard my dogs tree, and I ran to 'em as fast as I could. Sure enough when I came up, there was the bear in the crotch. My dogs were all lying down under him, and I don't know which was the most tired, they or the bear. I knew I had him, so I rested a minute, but I had to keep my dogs quiet, so old Betsey thundered. When he fell I was sorry, for he'd fought all day like a man and would have got clear but for me.

"He was pretty big, and it took me four turns on the log to bring him over the creek. When I'd packed the meat in a crotch the sun was most down, and the sky looked red and cold. I built a great fire of hickory and ash in a sheltered place and raised up a snow bank to keep the wind off the dogs. By that time in spite of everything I was most frozen. I recollected there was a mighty big spring not far off, and a notion struck me to go and get into it. When I got there I took off most of my clothes and put my legs in, and it felt so warm I sat right flat into it, and slid down so as to leave nothing out but my mouth and the upper part of my head. You don't know how good I did feel. When I think of it, I believe the happiest time I ever spent was while I was in that spring. It was harder getting out, but I went back to the fire, and piled up more wood, and dried my clothes, and stamped, and the dogs snuggled up close. By morning I was warm again, and my clothes were almost dry. Why some of my frolics haven't killed me, I don't know.

"The next morning the dogs were feeling lively as wildcats, and began snuffing, and at the word they were off. I thought it was turkeys, and sure enough, two gobblers rose over the harricane. I got 'em, and a very little time afterward I heard the dogs a barking. I found they were up the wrong tree, but they went on, barking again, and stopping, and still there was no bear. I was pretty mad then, and pulled out my horn and harked 'em on. We pushed through the harricane and past it for a long time till we came to an open prairie, and out there beyond my dogs there was about the biggest bear I ever saw. He looked like a big black bull. My dogs was afraid to attack him, and that's why they'd stopped so often, waiting for me to come up.

"I took the gobblers from my back and hung them on a sapling, and went after the bear, for the sight of him put new springs into me. The dogs got up to him and were soon in a roaring thicket. It was pretty close work for me to pick my way along. But the bear climbed up into a big black oak tree, and I crawled on till I got within about eighty yards of him. I put fresh priming in my gun and fired, and loaded again as quick as I could. He snorted at the first shot, but on the second he came tumbling down among the dogs. They piled in on him, and I heard old Grim cry out. I ran up with my tomahawk in one hand and my knife in the other. At that the bear let Grim go and fixed his eyes on me. I got back in all sorts of a hurry, for I knew if that bear got his paws on me he'd hug me too close for comfort. I called the dogs off, and fired again, and that was the end. He weighed no less than six hundred pounds, and I knew I'd have to make another day of it. I got him ready, packed part of the meat in the crotch of a tree, and in order to find him again I blazed saplings back to where the other bear was packed. The next day I got all the meat in the same place, and brought down some more gobblers.

"I guess my dogs know what they're about even when they seem to be barking up the wrong tree. Tomorrow we'll go after all that meat with the horses, and the boys can help."

There was silence, broken only by the snapping of the fire and the whir of Elizabeth's wheel. Robbie spoke. "But tomorrow's Christmas, and you said—"

"Sure enough. I said you might fire one of the Christmas guns."

The next morning at daybreak Robbie shot Betsey straight upward. John and William both fired off guns. Around the cabin there was a thunder of noise in the frosty air with light echoes. Christmas guns were echoing in many a clearing in the Southwest.

As the early sun sparkled yellow over the snow Crockett was off with John and William, all on horseback. "We must make haste," he said; "there's hardly a week's more bear hunting, and we'll need more meat and bear oil than we've got now, to last, and I must have more skins to trade." It took them the day to bring home all the game.

The Obion was now frozen fast. That night Crockett's friend from across the river was waiting for him at the cabin. He had come for a hunt and the next day they were off with William and John. They made a camp near the "harricane" with walls of snow, and soon the branches of the trees round about were hung with venison, wild turkeys, raccoons, bear meat, and skins. At the end of a week they had brought down seventeen bears.

Spring wheeled round, and after corn planting Crockett was off on horseback forty miles through cane and forest to the little settlement of Jackson, where he sold his peltry and bought coffee, sugar, powder, lead, and salt enough for several months' supplies. Back again at the Obion, he went ranging through the Shakes, sometimes on horseback, sometimes on foot. The boys were often with him. They skirted the great cracks still left by the earthquake, crossed low streams, and found Reelfoot Lake with its waters aglow with the yellow light of the great lilies. Fish floundered and jumped from the water, great catfish, gar, and others. Crockett was no fisherman, preferring to hunt, but since little time or patience was required for catches in the Reelfoot the boys brought home strings of great yellow catfish.

Once they passed a little hut at the head of the lake, thatched with moss and black with age, and caught a glimpse of the old hermit who lived there. "He's an old trapper," Crockett told the boys, "and there's stories about why he's hid himself in the woods all these years, but we won't bother him since he wants to be by himself. I know that feeling well."

Some days they went hunting bee trees, with clusters of yellow bottle gourds slung over their shoulders, tied with thongs of deerskin. Bee trees abounded in the Shakes. They could collect enough honey in a few days to fill all their gourds. Here and there they would pass a clearing where, as Crockett said, "some man's grubbed out a patch," but neighbors were still few and far between.

Once they all tramped over to the Mississippi, and stood on the high bluffs, watching until a small steamer came noisily round a bend.

Hunters now came into the country occasionally, riding

down from Kentucky or northern Tennessee. They sought out Crockett. The abundant fine peltry he had carried to Jackson had already given him farther fame. He was now spoken of as the great bear hunter of the Shakes—even as the great bear hunter of the West.

One cool November evening Crockett was sitting before the fire in his cabin, roasting potatoes and playing with his children when someone hallooed at the fence. Three strangers on horseback were there who said they had come to hunt bear and elk. They wanted Crockett to join them. "Light, strangers, and come in," said Crockett. Soon Elizabeth was cooking game and Crockett was pounding corn in a mortar for corncakes. The strangers spent the night.

The next morning, sounding his horn and harking on his dogs, he led the party through open woods. One of the strangers suddenly cried, "I'd give my horse to see a bear!"

"Well, give me your horse," said Crockett and he pointed to a bear three or four hundred yards ahead, feeding on acorns.

They all strained off, and the woods echoed as they came up. The bear hardly stirred until the dogs reached him. "He's buckling for it," shouted Crockett.

When the dogs reached him the bear turned and reared and boxed them right and left with his great paws. Howling, they came back. Two of them threw themselves upon him. The men were off their horses in an instant. Crockett had all he could do to keep the strangers from shooting; he feared they would shoot the dogs.

The dogs succeeded in getting the bear down. With a

single blow of his knife, Crockett killed him. The strangers perceived the skill and strength of the stroke. The dogs leapt upon the bear again and again. The strangers capered about almost as freely. "Blow me, if they didn't cut more capers jumping about than ever the dogs or the old bear did," said Crockett to Elizabeth. "I had fun just looking at 'em."

"Now we're all rested and ripe for the drive," Crockett told his new friends when all had mounted again and were riding toward the "harricane." "The fight with the bear just took the wiry edge off my dogs and they're in a better humor than ever."

Elk had been seen on the far side of the "harricane," and Crockett placed the strangers at stands before some open glades through which the elk might pass. Everything was quiet. Crockett leaned Betsey against a stump and lay down. Nearly an hour passed before Tiger opened. He howled once or twice, and Rattler gave a long howl, and the others joined in. One of the strangers shouted, "He's up, he's up!" Crockett seized his rifle. He could hear nothing but the continued roar of the dogs, coming toward him. A gun went off. The dogs stopped but not for long. They took a little back toward the glades where the strangers were posted, then circled way round to Crockett's left.

Crockett ran about a quarter of a mile toward them, then heard the dogs making a bend as though they were turning. He heard the bushes breaking lower down and started to run there. Just then two elk burst out of the cane, a buck and a doe, about a hundred and fifty yards below him. He waited until they reached an open space, then leveled, and fired. He brought down the buck.

"I don't know that I ever heard my dogs give such music," Crockett told the strangers. "Old hunter as I am, it made my hair stand right on end." Tiger lay against the buck. For a time the dog wouldn't let Crockett touch the great creature.

All at once the whole pack bounded up, growling, their hair stiff. "Perhaps it's the doe," said one of the strangers.

"Maybe," said Crockett doubtfully. "They act more as if 'twas a painter." Off they went at full cry. "Stranger, this will be hunting. Follow on!"

The eight dogs still sang out, clear as a bell. On several hundred yards through a glade in the cane Crockett saw a panther's tracks in the wet slash. Then they all entered the cane, following the dogs, pushing against the dry thick cracking stalks. All at once the dogs treed, and Crockett, peering over the brake into a gulley where an old beech stood, cried, "There he is on a limb, with his head pointed downward." It was the panther, tawny-dark against the gray limbs and trunk of the beech.

"He's more than a hundred yards off," cried one of the strangers.

For a moment there was silence, then the ring of the rifle, then the sound as Crockett crashed through the cane. The panther, struck, had leapt, and with the leap a dog cry arose, then another. The dogs had covered him, and he was about to deal out death to them with powerful strokes when Crockett ran up. Furiously the beast turned

Crockett pressed the muzzle of his gun against him as he came on, fired, and killed him.

"That took courage, Colonel," cried one of the strangers admiringly. But Crockett was looking at his dogs. They were badly mauled.

"I must stop for the painter skin, then we'll shoot only what comes our way as we go back."

On the return the dogs, though tired, started the doe elk, seen earlier, and one of the strangers was lucky enough to bring her down.

At night there was the usual talk after the hunt. "I suppose you've been in many a tight place," said one of the men to Crockett.

"I could tell you a thousand frolics I've had," he replied, "but perhaps this one will amuse you. I like bear hunting best of all. Bears is witty.

"It was evening and I was coming along, my pack horse loaded and my dogs following. All at once Soundwell held up his head and looked about, then rubbed his nose against a bush, and opened. I knew from the way he sung out that it was an old he-bear. The other dogs buckled in, and off they went like a thundergust right up a hollow. I tied my horse and set out after the dogs. The hollow up which the bear had gone made a bend, and I knew he would follow it, so I run across to head him. The sun was down now. 'Twas growing dark mighty fast, and 'twas cold: so I buttoned my jacket fast around me and run on. I hadn't gone far when I heard the dogs tack, and then come a tearing right down the hollow. Then I heard the old bear rattling through the cane, and the dogs like lightning after him. I dashed on and felt like I had wings, my dogs made such a roaring cry. They rushed by me and I harked them on. They all broke out again in their deep tones, and the woods echoed back and back and back with their voices.

" 'Twasn't long before they overhauled him and I could hear 'em fighting not far from me. Just before I got there the old bear made a break and got loose, but the dogs kept close up, and ever once in a while they stopped him and had a fight. I tried for my life to get up but before I'd get there he'd get loose. I followed him this way for three or four miles through briars and cane, and he deviled me mightily.

"Once I thought I had him. 'Twas so dark I couldn't tell him from a dog, and I started to go to him, but I found out there was a creek between us. How deep it was I didn't know, but it was too late to turn back, so I held up my rifle and walked right in. Before I got across the old bear got loose and shot for it through the cane. Well, I kept on, and once in a while I could hear my dogs fighting and baying just before me. I followed this way about four or five miles as near as I could guess, when the old bear couldn't stand it any longer and took a tree. I went up but at first it was so dark I could see nothing, but after looking about and getting the tree between me and a star I could see a very dark-looking place, and I raised old Betsey, and she lightened. Down came the old bear, but he wasn't much hurt.

"Of all the fights you ever see that one beat all. I had six dogs, and for nearly an hour they kept rolling and tum bling right at my feet. I couldn't see anything but an old white dog I had, but every now and then the bear made 'em sing out right under me. After a while bear, dogs, and all rolled down into a crack just before me, and I could hear 'em fighting like they was in a hole. I loaded Betsey and felt around in the hole with her till I got her agin the bear, and I fired, but I didn't kill him. Out of the hole he bounced, and the dogs fought harder than ever. They just formed a lump, rolling about, and presently they all went down into the hole again.

"My dogs began to sing out mighty often now. It had been the hardest fight I ever saw. I found out how the bear was laying, and I looked for old Betsey to shoot him again but I had laid her down somewheres and I couldn't find her, so I thought I would git down into the crack and kill him with my knife. I knew my bear was in a crack made by the shakes, but how deep it was and whether I could get out if I got in were things I couldn't tell. But my dogs would sing out as if they wanted help, so I let myself down into the crack behind the bear. Where I landed was about as deep as I am high, and I felt mighty ticklish. I couldn't see a thing in the world but I drew my knife and kept feeling about with my hands and feet till I touched the bear; this I did very gently. Then I got on my hands and knees and inched my left hand up his body with the knife in my right, though all the time he was twisting and turning with the dogs. I got pretty far up and then I plunged it into him. He sunk down, and for a minute there was a great struggle, but by the time I scrambled out overything was getting quiet. My dogs come out, one at a time, and laid down at my feet.

"I didn't know the direction of my tent so I determined to stay the night. I took out my flint and steel and raised a little fire, but the wood was so cold and wet it wouldn't burn much. I had sweated so after the bear that I began to get very thirsty and felt like I would die if I didn't get some water, so I went to look for the creek I had waded, and as good luck would have it I found the creek and got back to my bear. But from having been in a sweat all night I was now very chilly. I set to work again to build me a fire but all I could do wouldn't make it burn. The excitement I had been laboring under had all died away and I was so cold I felt very much like dying, but a notion struck me to get my bear up out of the crack, so down into it I went, and worked till I got myself into a sweat again, and just as I would get him up so high that if I could turn him over once he'd be out, he'd roll back. It began to hail mighty fine, but I kept on, and in about three hours I got him out.

"I came up almost exhausted. I laid down and soon fell asleep but 'twasn't long before I waked almost frozen. The wind sounded mighty cold as it passed along, and I called my dogs and made them lie upon me to keep me warm, but it wouldn't do. I got up and began to grope about in the dark, and the first thing I hit agin was a tree. It felt mighty slick and icy as I hugged it, so up I started, and I climbed that tree for thirty feet before I came to any limb, and then slipped down. It was warm work. How often I clomb that tree I never knew, but I was going up and slipping down and when day first began to break I was still going up that tree. As soon as it was cleverly light I saw it was a slim sweet gum, so slick that it looked like every varmint in the woods had been sliding down it for a month.

"Then I looked down the crack where I had taken my bear. Where we had all fought together was on a ledge in the crack, and just beyond, it went off so deep that I couldn't see to the bottom though all the morning light began to pour into it. It made me giddy to look at the dangers I'd escaped.

"Then I took old Betsey here, greased her and laid her away to rest a while. She's a mighty rough old piece but I love her, for she and I have seen hard times together. If I hold her right she always sends the ball where I tell her. She mighty seldom tells me a lie. My dogs and I have had many a high time of it, with old Betsey."

8

WRINGING THE TAIL OFF A COMET

Two or three times a year Crockett rode to the little settlement of Jackson to sell his furs and purchase supplies. Here he met men whom he had known in the Creek War; often he stayed for a day or two among them, exchanging stories at the tavern.

Travelers sometimes appeared there who were curious about this tall man in deerskin leggings and coonskin cap, known as the great bear hunter of the West. Sometimes they quizzed him. Crockett was friendly with strangers as a rule; even in a region where hospitality was dispensed with a free hand his warm welcome was famous. But he preferred not to be quizzed.

"I understand, Colonel Crockett," said a man in a tall beaver hat and a fawn-colored coat, "that you can tell by the scratches on the trees how tall a bear is that has just gone by, and you know how lean or fat he is by his tracks, and whether it's a he- or a she-bear."

"My littlest boy can tell those things."

The stranger was not to be snubbed. "I suppose you people down in the cane have plenty of bear steaks in winter," he remarked in a knowing and somewhat superior manner.

"We have plenty of bear steaks," said Crockett mildly. "I say, salt 'em with a hail storm, pepper 'em with buckshot, and broil 'em with a flash of lightning, and they make good eating."

The stranger laughed. "That's a quaint conceit. But what about the alligators? I understand the country down your way is alive with alligators. I suppose you often hunt them. It must be pretty dangerous work."

"The alligators is pretty thick all around, come spring when the dry lakes are full. A short way from our house there's a great deep pool where there's so many alligators that the whole circle's full as a tub of eels. They can sing proper about daybreak. I can hear 'em roaring like a horde of bulls. Sometimes they get atop our cabin, and once they knocked the chimney level with the roof and tore off all the bark and shingles. But I don't hunt 'em. I throw out a rope and snare 'em. Last spring I caught one thirty-seven feet long, and tamed him. In summer he comes up beside the cabin and we use him for a bench.

"Nothing but an alligator's tooth will do me to charge my Betsey. See it, stranger," and Crockett drew a great alligator's tooth from his buckskin bag. "But in my opinion bears makes better pets than alligators. My little boy brought a cub home in his pocket one day, and we tamed him. He's a big bear now and sits at the table like a man. We call him Death Hug, and I shouldn't wonder if he was smart enough to travel some day, and maybe go to Congress."

There was a restless movement among Crockett's companions in the tavern. Some had lifted their hands in front of their faces. One man choked a little. The stranger subsided, and presently left the room. A roar went up among the men.

"Crockett, you ought to go to Congress yourself!"

"Anyway, offer for the legislature."

"I like hunting too well to get into such things again," Crockett answered.

But not long after he had returned to his cabin a man came to him and told him that he had been made a candidate for the next legislature. He pulled out a newspaper from his pocket, and showed the announcement. This was in 1823.

"I think it's all a burlesque on me," Crockett told Elizabeth when the man had gone. "Some of those newspaper people probably think it would be pretty funny to have a hunter from the cane running for office. Let 'em have their fun! I'll push ahead and go through with it. Or stick."

When Crockett went around among the people of the widely spread district, he appeared as he did at home, in hunting shirt and fringed leggings. He spoke quietly.

"I've just crept out of the cane, to see what discoveries I could make among the white folks."

He talked with many who lived among canebrakes and were hewing out small patches for planting. Here and there he mounted a stump and made a plain, sensible speech, saying that if he were sent to the legislature he would try to see that people like themselves received their just due.

It happened that his opponent was a politician who had schemed mightily to secure the nomination. The voters balanced his character against Crockett's. They preferred Crockett. He was elected and served well as a representative, upholding fearlessly what he believed to be the rights of the hard working settlers of his district.

"Bushwhacker!" The name reached Crockett.

"I don't mind being called a bushwhacker. Bushwhackers pull themselves upstream as best they can, and sometimes they get there."

His speeches in the legislature were like his speeches on the stump, with occasional stories of hunting or life in the backwoods to illustrate the point.

Presently Crockett began to be talked of for Congress among the people of his district. "No," he said firmly, "I couldn't stand that. It's a step above my knowledge. I know nothing about matters in Congress."

In the second spring when Crockett returned from the legislature, times were hard in the Shakes. Coonskins failed to bring their usual price. Other furs brought less than the winter before. Crockett needed more money than when his children were younger. They were all growing fast, and the older ones had to be sent to school at Jackson. Though they could bind themselves out to work as he had done as a boy, men had to be found who would do their work on the farm, and these men had to be paid.

Staves were in good demand down the Mississippi. Crockett decided to hire some men to cut staves, joining in the work himself. He built two flatboats to take them down the river. Throughout the summer he worked at cutting staves and building the boats with the men and his own boys. In the autumn he stopped to hunt for a few weeks so that his family might be supplied for the winter. "To tell the truth," he said to Elizabeth, "I'd rather hunt than go down the river." But some thirty thousand staves had been cut, and the boats were ready. With some riverboatmen and a pilot he started down the Obion, and reached the Mississippi. He expected to go to New Orleans.

The Mississippi opened wide and treacherous. Great snags and sawyers loosed by the earthquake long ago still lay beneath its surface to impede boats or overturn them, and the current was swift. The men at the oars were strong and willing, and for a time the trip promised well, but the pilot was unskillful, and what was worse, he didn't know the river. Presently the forward boat came into churning white water. The boat trembled and almost whirled with the current. By good luck the chute was passed, but the two heavy boats were continually being warped out of their course. When at last they struck a piece of easy water and the two boats came close Crockett ordered them tied together, stern to bow, thinking that they could make better progress that way. This was a mistake, as he was willing to admit. "It made them so heavy and obstinate that it was next to impossible to do anything at all with them or even to guide them right in the river."

At night they tried to land, but they were unable to bring the boats ashore. On they went, in spite of every effort of the oarsmen and the pilot, and finally reached a great point of land reaching out into the river, called the Devil's Elbow. All worked hard and heavily to keep the boats from being overturned by the swift rush of the current, and at last they passed the Elbow safely. Below it they again tried to land. Through the darkness they saw the faint outlines of what appeared to be a little settlement. They shouted, thinking someone ashore could tell them where to come in. Men ran out with lights and shouted in answer, but the powerful current swept the boats on. The lights grew dim. The boats were out in the broad stream now with the Mississippi itself for pilot, the Big Old Great Strong River. Floating sideways, they were almost helpless.

Crockett, who was in the forward boat, went down into the cabin for a few moments, thinking what a hobble they were in. All at once he heard the boatmen running overhead in confusion, shouting, and felt the boat being pulled around as though the boatmen were bearing upon the oars with all their might. Then the boat went broadside over, and a great wash of water began pouring in upon him from the hatch. The only way out was a small hatch at the side that had been left open. As the boat turned, this was uppermost. Crockett thrust his arms and head through it and roared at the top of his voice. The boatmen came running. The hatch seemed much too small to let him pass, but through it lay his only chance of escape. "Pull!" he shouted. "It's neck or nothing." By a violent effort they pulled him through the hatch.

Crockett and the men were now perched on the square side of the great boat. The rearward boat had also overturned, and the boatmen there were riding on its side. Suddenly the forward boat plunged downward until the side where Crockett and the men were standing slanted as steeply as the top of a house. "Look ahead!" cried an old boatman. "She'll be sucked under!" All of them scrambled to the stern, succeeded in reaching the tow ropes, crossed them, and got aboard the rearward boat, which was riding at a perilous angle.

Ahead through the rush of darkness and the seething waters could be seen the dim outlines of what looked like a narrow island.

"It's a raft of drift timber," shouted the old boatman.

A great pile of trees and logs and bushes had been drawn together by the current. These rafts formed one of the greatest hazards of the river. The current boiled about them with deep suction. Already the forward boat was being drawn under. Most of it disappeared quickly.

Fastened by the tow rope, the rearward boat began tossing and heaving.

"Best make for the raft," said the old boatman.

One by one they crawled over the tow ropes to the forward boat, whose stern was still partly above water, jammed against the raft. In the murky darkness they crept along until they reached the overhanging driftwood. Finding slippery footholds, one by one they landed safely.

All night there was a rattle and slap of loosened staves, and the chug and push of the flatboats. Underneath the raft the forward boat began to pound. "If this keeps up it'll rack this driftwood to pieces," said the old boatman. There was a ripping, tearing noise, and the raft settled a little. "I believe the first boat's going, or gone," exclaimed Crockett. No light showed on the water or on shore, and a storm was threatening. They had all lost everything except the little they had on. The raft began to drift.

"Do you know," said Crockett later, "while I was sitting there, floating about on that raft, I felt happier and better off than I had ever felt in my life before! For I had just made a most marvelous escape. I forgot everything else but that. I felt prime, no matter what was to happen."

The next morning at sunrise they saw only the wide brown waste of the river, covered with staves. The two flatboats had disappeared.

In the distance rose a sharp whistle. A black crest of smoke rose over the Devil's Elbow. Then round the bend came a little steamboat. They hailed her, and a skiff was sent over. Crockett and the men were taken aboard. Passing the high knobs of the Chickasaw Bluffs, they landed at Memphis. Here a merchant whom Crockett knew let them have fresh clothing and shoes and a little money.

Someone on the wharf at Memphis declared that he had seen the two overturned flatboats floating down the river.

Crockett took passage to Natchez, hoping to discover them along the way. Later he heard that they had gone aground on the other side, above Memphis, but on the trip up the river he failed to sight them. "This is the last of my boats," he said cheerfully. The long work of the summer was lost.

When he reached home he found that the story of his adventure had traveled before him.

"We heard you went straight down to the bottom of the river and stayed there when the boat turned over," said his smallest boy, George. "And when you came up you'd traveled all over the river bottom. A man said you weren't even wet when you came up. He said you could run faster, dive deeper, stay under longer, and come up drier than any man in all creation."

"I reckon I looked like a pretty cracklin' when they dragged me out of that hatch-hole, but I wasn't dry. I was wet all over. What else did he say?"

"He said you could eat up a wildcat, and hold a buffalo out to drink, look a painter to death, take a steamboat on your back, stand three streaks of lightning without dodging, and put a rifle ball through the moon."

"Anything more?"

"He said you were the yaller blossom of the forest, and when you stood up for a fight you jumped in the air and cracked your heels and crowed like a rooster, and neighed like a stallion. Let's hear you."

"Pretty soon. I reckon I *can* make a sound like most any creature that ever drew breath if I'm a mind to. But I haven't had any fights. Not one. It's riverboatmen that jump in the air and crack their heels when they're getting ready for a tussle. Where did all these tales come from?"

"They're spread out all over the district, Davy," said Elizabeth. "And people say you're going to run for Congress. There was a squib in one of the papers about it. Calling you the gentleman from the cane."

"That'll be old Cambric Ruffle at work again."

"Cambric Ruffle" was the name he had given to a member of the legislature who wore, as Crockett thought, finicking fine clothes. "I know him pretty well. He's trying to put me down, calling me the gentleman from the cane. I don't mind the tales and talk, but that makes me mad all over. Well, I've been spoken of for Congress afore now, and maybe I'll try it!"

The Western District, as it was called, was still wild. Settlers were entering it slowly but their cabins were still far apart, and thieves roamed through the country. Murrell, who had been branded as a horsethief, had now established a hidden base somewhere in an all but impenetrable stretch of forest and was engaged in Negro running, counterfeiting, and again in horse stealing. Confederates had joined him. The gang often moved far to the south into sparsely settled portions of Mississippi and across the river into Arkansas. They were said to have discovered hidden caves along the Mississippi for storing their loot.

Though the Western District thus became notorious the settlers there took life much as had their forbears who had come over the Blue Ridge when eastern Tennessee was haunted by hostile Indians. There were frolics, and Crockett and Elizabeth were not too old to attend them. These frolics were far from sedate. Fiddle tunes flew faster and faster. One of these was the "Forked Deer" which took its name from a crooked rapid river flowing into the Mississippi not far south of Crockett's cabin. Many of these tunes borrowed names from wild places. There was the "Knob Dance"—named for the great knobs in western Tennessee, once held by the Chickasaws. There was "Natchez-under-the-Hill," for the wicked village of the Mississippi River front. "Rocky Mountains" doubtless induced high steps. There were dance-tunes that sounded like the baying of hounds in full cry. And lively Irish reel tunes were played, like "Miss McCloud."

So altogether the Shakes was considered a savage and fantastic region by sedate town-dwellers of Tennessee, and the notion of sending a bear hunter from the district to Congress became a joke that was propounded with many variations. More quips on the subject appeared in the newspapers. But for two years Crockett had been riding among his distant neighbors in that time of leisure when "craps were laid by"—between midsummer and harvest. These neighbors were small landowners like himself for the most part. And he often ran across companions of the Creek War. In 1827 when a congressional election again came round he decided to run.

Two other candidates appeared for the office of representative in Crockett's district, men of some wealth and position. When a meeting was arranged, often all three would speak from the same platform—or stump. Crockett' speeches were invariably short. He talked plainly about matters then before the country. The other two candidates disregarded him altogether in their speeches, as if they did not credit the fact that the bear hunter meant to go to Congress. In their speeches they answered each other. They might have been the only men on the ticket.

Once when one of them was making a long harangue in a little settlement a flock of guinea fowl wandered near the platform, chattering noisily in their shrill key. The speaker was greatly confused, stopped, and asked to have them driven away. When his harangue was ended Crockett walked forward and spoke. "Well, Colonel, you're the first man I ever saw that really understands the language of the fowls. You never mentioned me at all in your speech though you talked about the other man boldly enough. But my good friends the guinea fowl came up, crying 'cr-cr-kt.'"

Here Crockett imitated the shrill cry of the guinea fowl, at the same time shaping the sounds so that they said his name—"Cr-cr-kt-kt, Cr-kt-kt-tt."

The crowd roared. Crockett's opponent was confused, and had no reply.

"That story will circulate all over like smoke," said one of Crockett's friends. "He was as bothered as a fly in a tar-pot."

The story was freely told, with variations. Sometimes it was crickets that creaked and chirped "Cr-k-tt." Sometimes it was bullfrogs in a neighboring pond with a hoarse gut-tural, "Cro-o-ck-ett-tt."

When all the speeches had been made, the barbecues

held, the votes counted, Crockett was found to have won by a considerable majority.

"Why is it," he asked Elizabeth after the count was made, "why is it I'm always a getting into such a hotchpotch and confusion when there's nothing I like better than to live right here in the Shakes where I can go off in the woods alone and stay as long as I like?"

"Sometimes I think there's two Davy Crocketts," Elizabeth answered sagely.

"I believe there's ten when I hear all those big stories," said Robbie.

"I should think you'd rather hunt any day than go to Congress," said William.

Crockett turned his career in Congress into a gusty adventure. He attracted attention at once. He was not wearing his hunter's garb, but he quickly became known in Washington as the "coonskin congressman." No one at all like him had appeared in office; he aroused great curiosity. His tall figure was striking. His casual speech was often repeated because of its pithy center. Tall talk was easily attributed to him.

On his way to Washington he was said to have been accosted at a tavern by a stranger. "Hurrah for Adams!" said the stranger. "You'd better say hurrah for hell and praise your own country," said Crockett in reply, according to the story. Said the stranger, "Who are you?" Said Crockett "I'm David Crockett, fresh from the backwoods, half horse, half alligator, a little touched with snapping turtle. I ca wade the Mississippi, leap the Ohio, ride a streak of lightning, slip without a scratch down a honey locust, whip my weight in wildcats, hug a bear too close for comfort and eat any man opposed to Jackson!"

Such stories were printed in many eastern newspapers of the time, and they all stressed Crockett's loyalty to Jackson. He had entered Congress as part of the Jackson contingent.

Washington must have presented a bewildering number of new sights and strange people to Crockett. But he seems to have gone his own way from the first, and to have made his own judgments. He drove straight to a salient point which was to impress him throughout his congressional career. An immense amount of talk was going on—too much talk, he thought—too many dull speeches, with nothing done.

He said so. "Some men," he exclaimed, "seemed to take pride in saying a lot about nothing. Their tongues go like windmills whether they have grist to grind or not. Others just listen. Some members of Congress do nothing at all for their pay but just listen, day in and day out. But I wish I may be shot if I don't think they earn every penny, considering most of the speeches. That is, provided they don't go to sleep. No one can imagine what dreadful hard work it is to keep awake and listen to what's said most of the time. Splitting gum logs in August is nothing beside it."

At first Crockett was awkward in address on the floor of the House. His enemies declared that he never learned the rules of debate, but this was not true. Because of his experience in the Tennessee legislature he knew the outlines of the proper procedure. He could make an able, witty speech, and he quickly learned to seize advantages in argument. At times he amused the House with a free use of backwoods humor, but he could curb this in the interest of measures he wished to promote. His printed speeches show that in the difficult art of rebuttal he was easy, often far-sighted. By his second term he found himself in the thick of more than one battle.

A great issue had taken new shape, that of the disposal of public lands. Before the first David Crockett had come over the Blue Ridge, even before the Revolution, men had followed in the wake of the fur-traders to seize great tracts of valuable land in the wilderness, with the prospect that this would be greatly enhanced in value when other men should come to the same parts of the country and settle there. The actual settlers who followed were often obliged to take inferior tracts. Land titles were juggled, and men who had cleared land with great effort were often deprived of this by chicanery.

In the Western District of Tennessee from which Crockett came, this situation had become acute. Warrants for land in Tennessee had been granted long before to Revolutionary soldiers from North Carolina—fairly enough, as a reward, but with no stipulation that these men themselves should live on the land and cultivate it. Most of the warrants had been sold to speculators, who had claimed the best tracts in the District. Settlers had also come, and had taken up claims to which they believed themselves entitled, clearing the land on which they lived of cane and timber. The speculators had then come out to the District and, as Crockett said, had "ransacked, picked, and culled the country till everything valuable has been located."

Many settlers had been dispossessed. Some of them had then moved to what Crockett called "patches and refuse scraps and shapeless fragments of land" in barren or inaccessible parts of the District—scraps that the speculators had scorned or overlooked. Now they were being driven from these by the burden of a heavy and—as Crockett thought—highly unfair tax. An expensive survey had been made of boundaries in this region, and the cost of it had been spread over the District.

"I have seen the last blanket of an honest, industrious, poor family sold under the hammer to pay for that survey!" said Crockett in a speech before the House. "And most of that land's so poor it wouldn't even raise a fight!"

Further, the title of the farmers to these small "refuse scraps" was now in question. The majority of the Tennessee delegation wanted to sell these at a price and under terms which Crockett knew the poor settlers of his District could not meet. He was shrewd enough to see that this action would lead to further speculation, which would bring wealth to men who had never turned a furrow or built a rail fence, at the sacrifice of the improvements which the settlers had laboriously added. Crockett proposed a low price and an extended term for payment. He was downright in his denunciation of the speculators. His argument was warm and impassioned on behalf of these, his poorer neighbors—"these men of the western waters, these men who have broken the cane."

"Their little all," he cried, "is to be wrested from them for the purposes of *speculation,* and a swindling machine is to be set up to strip them of what little the surveyors and the warrant holders have left them. It shall never be said that I sat by in silence!" He warmly insisted that the speculators had already taken advantage of the natural alarm in the district and had perpetrated the grossest frauds and impositions.

Crockett achieved a homely statesmanship. His bill dealing with this question was carefully thought out and well phrased, and he supported it with a wealth of ready argument.

The question was fiercely debated. The Tennessee legislature had given a mandate to the congressmen from the state not to let the lands go at a low price; and most of them followed this. Then, the powerful influence of the administration was thrown against Crockett's proposals. Jackson had himself been a speculator in land on a large scale from an early day. Consideration of the bill was repeatedly postponed. Crockett finally said that he "would rather it were taken up and rejected than that it should thus be sported with." Support came to him mainly from Whigs of the East. His bill was defeated, as was an important amendment of his to another measure bearing on the same question. He won a few concessions for his people. The fixing of land titles in the Western District was postponed for ten years and when this occurred the actual settlers were given right of preëmption, as result of Crockett's blunt, unwavering stand. He won nothing tangible for the principle at stake.

Perhaps in 1829 or 1830 few men could have gauged the force of the blow that had been dealt to this principle. "Equal opportunity" was a phrase on many lips. But in a most vital relationship, that of an eager people to the new, rich land, equal opportunity did not exist. Crockett himself could not have judged of the final results of this blow. Few if any in his time could have prophesied the rapid expansion of the country. Few seemed able to perceive the relation of an equitable land ownership to the purposes of a democracy. None the less Crockett stands head and shoulders above the average thinker of the time, even above many in high places, because of his grasp of a fundamental principle and his willingness to fight for it. The cause was lost, but it was a great cause.

When Crockett had been a member of the Tennessee legislature some of the preliminaries of the question had been debated, and Crockett had then stood firmly for the rights of the actual settler. Politically he had little to gain and everything to lose by opposing the dominant party in his state. It took courage and honesty to do so. Jackson was riding into a high popularity, and the easier course would have been to follow.

Again Crockett clashed with Jackson, and again the issue had to do with the disposal of land—the land possessed by the five tribes of the Southwest, the Cherokees, Creeks, Choctaws, Chickasaws, and Seminoles.

Some of the treaties by which these tribes came into possession of their lands had been made soon after the Revolution. The treaty to which Big Warrior referred at the end of the Creek War had been made by Washington. By this and others the lands were given to the Indians to hold "forever." In the treaty which Jackson had concluded with the Creeks at the end of the Creek War the promises of security, ownership, and protection had been solemnly renewed.

But now these Indian lands were discovered to be very rich. Gold had been discovered in certain sections; some of the best soil for growing cotton in the entire South was to be found there. Without law, without sanction, white settlers had begun to invade the Indian lands, often dispossessing the owners by force. Armed clashes had taken place. Authorities in the given states—Florida, Georgia, Alabama, Mississippi—generally wished the Indians removed. Some disorder existed in the Indian villages, but probably no more than had appeared in most new white settlements. Large numbers of Indians were prosperous, law-abiding citizens. On the whole the members of the five tribes had shown themselves eager to adopt the ways of white men.

Perhaps as commanding general in the Creek War Jackson had lost sympathy with the Indians, even though friendly Creeks and Cherokees had served him well. Political pressure doubtless played a part. His conviction had crystallized, and he was sponsoring a measure for the removal of the five tribes to new territory beyond the Mississippi, and he pressed for the passage of the necessary bill.

Davy Crockett was both ardent and outspoken against

this measure, and he stood alone in his position among the members from Tennessee. "I know I stand alone from my state," he said. "None of my colleagues agree with my sentiment, but if I should be the only member of the House who voted against the bill and the only man in the United States who disapproved of it, I would still vote against it, and it would be a matter of rejoicing till the day I died that I did so."

He was charged with not representing his constituents in this matter, and it was true that most of them were either hostile to the cause of the Indian, or indifferent to it. "I don't wish to represent my fellow citizens unless I can act according to my conscience," he answered.

"A treaty is the highest law of the land," said Crockett flatly. "But there are those who do not find it so. They want to juggle with the rights of the Indian and fritter them away. It's all *wrong*. It's not justice. I would rather be an old coon dog belonging to a poor man in the forest than belong to any party that will not do justice to all. These are the remnants of a once powerful people, and they must be fairly treated."

In the argument Crockett cited his friendship with the Chickasaws in the Western District; he had talked with many Cherokees on the question and was in close touch with John Ross, a chief spokesman of that tribe. Almost as a whole the five tribes were opposed to removal.

When it seemed probable that the bill would be passed, Crockett demanded an investigation of the character of the lands to which it was proposed to send these Indians. They had never been nomadic; all had lived in villages. They were no longer hunters or warriors: yet the new country across the Mississippi—the Indian Territory—was preyed upon by warlike, nomadic bands of hunters, the Comanches, Sioux, Osages, Pawnees. The country was totally different from that to which the five tribes were accustomed, requiring different forms of cultivation.

At a last stand in the argument, Crockett urged that if the tribes wished to emigrate after all the conditions were made clear to them, then a full and careful plan for their removal should be drawn up.

In the East and North strong opposition to Jackson's Indian bill arose. The Society of Friends opposed the measure. Eminent lawyers were opposed to it. Crockett's speeches were widely discussed, and one of them—homely, warm, impetuous—found a place in a volume of others on the same subject by notable men of the time. Edward Everett was one of them. But the bill—and other measures related to it—was passed. Before long the great forced migration of the tribes was under way. The Indians were forced to follow what they called the "Trail of Tears." No survey of the new lands was made, no careful plans developed such as Crockett had urged. The removal was haphazard. Many Indians were robbed of all their possessions at the outset by greedy whites who were at hand, ready to seize their farms and houses. The journey was often pressed in heartless haste. Many thousands of Indians died before they reached the new territory. The outcome makes a dark page in American history.

When the Indian bill came up some of Crockett's friends urged him not to persist in his opposition to Jackson. "I'll wear no man's collar," he answered roundly. "Long ago I fixed on a motto. That motto is, 'Be always sure you're right, then go ahead.' I follow it to this day, and I shall always follow it, come what will. The President is wrong about the Indians, and I know it."

The adoption of lost causes is not the surest means of personal advancement. Crockett's position on the land question and on the Indian bill created a strong rebound against himself. The Jackson forces were uppermost in Tennessee and in the nation. The people of the Western District had remained uninterested in the fate of the Indian; and as to the land question, they could only see that Crockett had been unsuccessful. He sent a printed circular to the voters of the District explaining his position on all important matters before Congress during his previous term, and he canvassed the territory with speeches. But the organized opposition was strong. He was defeated in 1831.

During the next two years Crockett farmed and hunted in the Shakes as he had done before. In open winter weather or when "the craps were laid by" in August he rode around the District, talking over questions of the time with the people there, discovering their interests and ideas. In 1833, though the same opponents were in the field, he was again elected to the House.

In this interval his personal popularity in Washington had greatly increased. Crockett always carried himself easily, and he was welcome among many groups. The Whigs admired him because he was a thorn in the side of the Democrats, but he was widely liked for his wit and character as well.

Stories were told of his entering the White House, when a lackey cried, "Make way for Colonel Crockett!" "Colonel Crockett can make way for himself," said Davy dryly. He had been piqued by a report that he could not behave himself properly, and was said to have procured written testimony that he had done so, sending this back to his constituents.

He knew that he was constantly being ridiculed by his enemies as the "coonskin congressman." Once after a heated debate he received a challenge to a duel from another member of Congress. Crockett regarded duels as silly. "Tell him I'll fight," he said to the messenger. "Since he challenged I suppose I can pick the weapons. Tell him we'll fight with bows and arrows!"

A congressman conspicuous for noisy oratory said to him in a public place, "I presume, Colonel Crockett, that when you *walked* to Washington you met a great many wild animals on the way, and I presume you killed them all."

Crockett had traveled to Washington by stage.

"I started out with a few hurricane speeches tied up in an alligator hide," he replied promptly, "and on the way I put down my bundle to hunt a bear. I found him, and killed him, and I was roasting some steak for my dinner when I heard a great snorting and scattering amongst the leaves, and there was a panther making off with my bundle of patriotism! I knew 'twould never do to lose it, for how should I get along in Washington when others got off all their windy talk?

"My bundle was pretty light and the panther went off with it at a great rate. But of course I put after him like a shooting star and after a wrestle I got it back again. Then I sat down and finished my bear steak. I got to Washington with my bundle and finally I let loose my speeches. That was the time of the big wind."

There were times when Davy could not resist playing the uncouth backwoodsman. Like many men of the frontier and many congressmen he was something of an actor. Once he went traveling in the western part of Virginia with Matthew St. Clair Clarke of Pennsylvania, Clerk of the House, a scholar, a wit, and himself "a prodigy of story telling." The two stopped at a public house over night, and in the morning they found a traveling menagerie in the village. Crockett at once insisted that he must have "a peep at the critters." The tent containing the menagerie was already crowded with country people when Clarke and Crockett arrived. No sooner had Davy reached the center of the tent than he tipped his hat on the side of his head and sang out in a loud voice, "Is that 'ere hyena for sale?" "No," answered the keeper. "Well, mister," Crockett asked, "what would be the damages if I was to kill him?" The keeper nervously answered that no money would purchase him. "But dam-me, Mr. Keeper," said Davy, "I want to grin at him just to let you see the fur fly." The hyena's grin was of course famous; because of it people came to see hyenas. And the many stories of Davy's grin, which could bring down a coon from a treetop, had been well circulated.

Setting himself against the tent pole Crockett began going through maneuvers of the arms, contortions of the face, with a wild grin. The keeper began to be alarmed for fear Crockett would really kill the hyena. Anxiety spread to the spectators. At last Crockett was persuaded to let the hyena alone, but he immediately declared that he must fight the lion, and took off his coat. When he walked toward the cage with an air of solemn determination, the spectators rushed out pellmell, carrying with them part of the tent.

During the two years of Crockett's retirement in the Shakes a play had been put on called "The Lion of the West" and also another, similar to this, "The Kentuckian," whose hero in each case was a certain Colonel Nimrod Wildfire, a hunter in coonskin cap and deerskin leggings, who talked much as Crockett talked—or as people said he talked —or as at times he permitted himself to talk. The author, Paulding, declared that he had had no intention of portraying Crockett, but the great audiences that flocked to see the play in the East were firm in their belief that Wildfire was Crockett. The part was played by James Hackett, who in Shakespearean rôles had pleased many fastidious playgoers.

When Hackett took a benefit in Washington during Crockett's third term, he announced that at the particular request of Colonel Crockett he would appear in the character of Nimrod Wildfire. The house was crowded to the ceilings. At seven Crockett came in, and was escorted to a front seat by the manager. Hurrahs and shouts made a great din. "Go ahead! Go ahead!" "I wish I may be shot!" "Music! Music!" "Let's have Crockett's March!" A new march had been composed in Davy's honor. It was played, and when Hackett came on in the familiar hunting garb he bowed first to the audience, then to Crockett, who bowed in return. It was a hilarious gala evening.

But if Crockett was often occupied with filling the part of backwoodsman, he was also as much engaged with public affairs as he had been during his first two terms in Congress, though few measures before the House touched him as closely as had the land bill and the Indian bill. He was now a confirmed anti-Jackson man, and voted consistently against the administration on the vexed question of the bank and the deposits. He was still outspoken as to the ways of politicians. "Their fair promises to their people are worth about as much as a flash in the pan when you have a shot at a fat bear," he declared. "I notice a good many speakers here put in handsome flourishes about the heroes who fought and bled for our liberties, and the times that tried men's souls. Then they frank their frothy flourishes back to their districts, and that's all the frankness the people ever get."

He discovered that political bargaining was going on between members from the East and those from the West, and he criticized this plainly and shrewdly from the floor of the House. Questions of internal improvement were to the fore. It was proposed to build roads which Crockett, who knew the country, thought impracticable. He said so. He was not opposed to the spread of education, as his apponents declared, but he was candid in opposing lavish grants of land to certain colleges. In education, as in the matter of land ownership, he wanted equality of opportunity.

Crockett gave himself with genuine eagerness to the interests of his constituents. Many of his brief speeches show that his main concern was for the small farmer, the hopeful new settler. And he kept in constant touch with his own people by letter. In these years he lived in a whirl of letter-writing, to leading Whigs, to unknown individuals who asked him for introductions, to his large and growing circle of friends, to his family. As a writer he had made an extraordinary progress from the days in southern Tennessee when he had laboriously practised the art in order to keep his records as a magistrate. His spelling and punctuation were always lawless, but his script steadily improved. He finally wrote a bold clear hand.

At the same time he mastered the art of putting his thoughts on paper in natural form. His letters were easy often witty; scarcely one lacked some direct, personal touch He was becoming no less adroit with other writing. The circulars which he sent to the voters of the Western Distric in 1827 and 1831 contain portions which read like officia reports and were doubtless inserted by some friendly ad viser. But the main substance was Crockett's; it tallie closely with the style of his oral debates, and shows the stamp of a fresh, firm, original style.

In an unstudied fashion Crockett had achieved a qualit

that belongs to all significant writing. He could communicate on paper; his words had the impact of lively speech. It was hardly strange that he should set down the story of his life at this time. Men who liked his salty talk were always urging him to tell them of his adventures. The notion took shape in Crockett's mind because of this warm persuasion, and also because a book appeared that purported to tell his history. This was the anonymous "Sketches and Eccentricities of Col. David Crockett of West Tennessee." This book was inaccurate, and at many points its purpose seemed to be that of ridicule. But the writer had evidently been in close touch with Crockett and had included many stories as he had told them. Davy Crockett had become a highly popular subject in the East as well as the West; the newspapers of the day were full of small squibs and news items about him. The book at once had a large circulation.

Naturally Crockett resented its appearance. He resolved to write his own story and did so. In 1834 his first book was published, his "Narrative of the Life of David Crockett, of the State of Tennessee, Written by Himself." He said candidly that a friend helped him to "classify the matter," and the manuscript was sent to the printer in another hand than his own, Thomas Chilton's, doubtless because of Davy's uncertain spelling. Chilton was a member of the House from Kentucky who shared some of Crockett's convictions: on important measures they often voted together. A few alterations seem to have been made in the book by Chilton, but it was essentially Crockett's. Its success prompted him to write another.

In the spring of 1834 he started on a long tour, and he put down his observations along the way in "An Account of Col. Crockett's Tour to the North and Down East." The journey was generally considered to be a political affair, undertaken in the campaign against Van Buren. Crockett made a number of political speeches against "the little red fox," but the tour turned into a continuous ovation for himself. Great crowds turned out to see him. Everywhere he was offered a lavish hospitality. His account of the journey shows as much pleasure as though he had found himself in new hunting country.

From Baltimore he traveled down Chesapeake Bay by steamer and took a great fancy to the captain. "A good fellow he is, bowing and scraping to the ladies, nodding to the gentlemen, cursing the crew, and keeping his right eye broadcast all the time. 'Let's go,' he said, and we walked off in prime style right down Chesapeake Bay, and in a very short run we came to a place where we had to get aboard the railroad cars.

"This was a clean new sight for me. About a dozen big stages were hung onto one machine. After a good deal of fuss we got seated, and moved slowly off, the engine wheezing as though she had the tizzick. By and by she began to take short breaths, and away we went a blue streak. It was nigh dark, and we went whizzing along with sparks flying in all directions. At Delaware City we got into another boat to take us to Philadelphia."

The captain of the boat hoisted three flags to show that Crockett was aboard. When they reached the wharf this was black with people, who threw their hats in the air and cheered for Crockett as he came down the gangplank. A barouche was waiting, drawn by four horses, to which he was formally escorted. As he was driven through the city more and more crowds appeared; the windows were full of people. "This is all very well," said Crockett, "but I most think I'd rather be in the wilderness with my gun and dogs than to be attracting all this fuss."

None the less he had a certain amount of fun out of it. "Those Philadelphians are eternally cutting up jokes," he declared, "so we had a high night of it at the tavern."

"And in the morning all up and down the street, such a scrubbing of steps and even the pavements, you never saw!"

He was waited on by a party of gentlemen who presented him with a gold seal for his watch with an engraving on the stone of two horses running at full speed, and over them the words, *"Go Ahead."* They told him that a fine rifle was to be given him, made precisely according to his wishes. He mentioned the weight and length he liked, and before he left the handsomely mounted and finely finished rifle was presented to him. That evening he spoke to five thousand people out of doors at the Exchange.

When Crockett reached New York on the first of May he was astonished to find hundreds moving. "It would take a good deal to get me out of my log house," he said, "but there most people move once a year anyway. And in that city they're forever tearing down buildings and putting up new ones. A man I talked to pointed to the house he was leaving, and it was a fine house, but in a few hours there

were men on top of it, and before evening there was daylight through it. John Jacob Astor is going to build a great
tavern where it stood.

"Then we went down to a place called Five Points where
the buildings are little old frame houses and look like some
country village. All the houses have cellars, and people live
in them. And such fiddling and dancing nobody ever saw,
black and white people all hug-'em-snug-'em, happy as lords
and ladies. Some of 'em were sitting round in a ring with a
jug of liquor between 'em. I thought I'd rather risk myself
amongst wild Indians than amongst those creatures at night.

"There's too many people in New York, and too close
together. But I tell you one thing. I went to the theater and
saw the prettiest play-acting lady in the world. She was
like a handsome piece of changeable silk." This was Fanny
Kemble.

From New York to Providence Crockett traveled by
boat and saw many sights that were new to him.

"When the sun rose in the morning it come up like a
ball of fire out of the water, and looked for all the world
as if it had been just made for the first time.

"Over on the shore of New England the country was all
laid off in little fields, divided by stone fences.

"When I took the stage from Providence to Boston and
began to ride through New England, I thought what a
mighty hard land it is all hereabouts! It seems as though
the whole face of the earth had been covered with stones
They've got them strung up in fences, as many as they

can, but they won't stay picked. Every time they plow, a
new crop comes up."

Crockett liked Boston, and was warmly received there.
'It's a long-necked village, like a squash or a calabash. They
took me to Faneuil Hall, a great big place, and told me this
was the cradle of liberty. I reckon old King George thought
they were thundering fine children that were rocked in it,
and a good many of them. I saw many people, and went to
their houses. They appear to me to live in New England
more snugly and to have more kind feelings toward each
other than any people I ever saw.

"Before I started back, I went to Lowell, and visited the
mills, and saw them make calico in beautiful colors, scarlet and blue and purple. Why, it was wonderful, the way
they could turn out that calico so fast. It almost come up
to the story of the old fellow who walked into a patent machine with a bundle of wool under his arm and came out
at the other end with a new coat on!"

Crockett was vastly and candidly pleased by the new
friends he had made and by the warmth with which he had
been received among strangers. Some months earlier he had
been talked about as a candidate for president, at first
perhaps jokingly. The talk was now repeated, and undoubtedly he was dazzled by the idea. On his journey west
through Pennsylvania and by steamer down the Ohio to
Louisville, crowds of people turned out to see him in towns
along the way. He made speeches in Pennsylvania, Ohio,
Kentucky. He was fêted at banquets. It was a triumphal
journey. "Go where I will," he exclaimed, "everybody

seems anxious to get a peep at me. I can't tell why it is nor in what it is to end."

In later years it was said that the Whigs gave Crockett his singular position, as part of their campaign against Jackson. Probably they added momentum to his fame, but for the most part Crockett himself had created it, by his character, by his racy talk. This hunter from the West had appeared in the public view at a moment when the American imagination was alight in New England, in the back country of the South, and in the West. It was a time of myth-making: great comical myths were being invented about people and about the land. Frontiersmen were not a dour race. Crockett had created myths by his high talk and his stories. In turn, he became something of a myth then and afterward. It was the comical, irrepressible, legendary Crockett who had captured the popular fancy.

Even now as he was traveling homeward tall stories about him were circulated. People said that once when he was traveling up the Ohio in a steamboat the machinery stopped, and the boat began drifting with the current so Crockett got out and towed her upstream, and once started he took her up over the Falls. And they were saying that he was going to wring the fiery tail off the comet.

In the year 1835 all the world was awaiting Halley' comet, the great comet with an aurora-like flame and a long streaming tail of fire that had been seen long ago by the Egyptians, and again when William the Conqueror landed in England. Its appearance was thought to accompany or foretell marvelous, strange events. Many feared its advent which was to occur in early November. Some believed that the comet's fiery tail would sweep over the entire world, bringing death and destruction. Suddenly the story went round that Crockett was to mount the highest peak in the Alleghany Mountains and wring off its tail as it passed and prevent this destruction.

When some strange or comic happening occurred people would say, "I tell you, it's nothing to Crockett!"

In the midst of all this lively glory came a harsh blow. At the end of the summer Crockett stood again for election. But he had failed to measure the depth of envy and dislike that he had created. Sectional prejudices were rife. His journey to New England was used against him. The concerted force of the Jacksonian party in Tennessee was brought into opposition. Many small schemers were at work; and whatever his faults, Crockett had no aptitude for scheming. It was a savage campaign. Crockett's opponent was Adam Huntsman, whom he had met before in the political field. Huntsman had a wooden leg. Crockett called him Old Timbertoes, and accomplished a few explosive practical jokes at his expense. Huntsman's tactics were on much the same level. The issues at stake for the small farmers, for the struggling frontiersmen, went down in a welter of jokes and personalities, and Crockett was defeated by a narrow margin.

He was by no means friendless; soon after the election a public dinner was given in his honor at the Planter's Hotel in LaGrange, and later testimony shows that he commanded the confidence of men of substantial character in Tennessee. But he had decided to abandon politics. "I have announced through the news papers that I never expect to offer my name again to the public for any office," he wrote in accepting the invitation to the dinner. "I hope to spend the evening in a social manner, leaving politics out of the question."

Crockett had reached a turning point. In the six or seven years just past his entire course had been changed; he could now hardly return to hunting and farming in the Shakes. All his life he had been on the move, and he had repeatedly gone on from one frontier to another. He made a quick decision. "I'm going to Texas," he said.

Encouraged by the Mexican authorities many small bands of Americans had settled in Texas; but dissensions between these settlers and the Mexican government had steadily increased as that government was changed by the uncertainties of civil war and revolution. The Republic of Coahuila and Texas had been formed but had proved unstable. Rumbling threats of an invading Mexican army were heard. Skirmishes along the border had created further tension. The Texas Revolution broke out on October 2, 1835. Austin issued an appeal that was repeated over the country, calling for volunteers in the cause of the Republic. Houston issued an appeal. Talk of purchasing Texas had long been heard in the United States; now annexation was freely discussed. Texas—or "the Texas," as it was then sometimes called—was said to be fabulously rich.

"I'll be off," said Crockett. "There's something about

this which makes me feel I must be in it. The Aurora Borealis is nothing more nor less than the whole of the North Pole poking up with a colored flare to get admission among the stars of the Union, and I reckon the prairies of Texas are doing the same. Perhaps in the end I can carve out new land for ourselves."

His oldest son was now teaching in an academy; his other boys were grown or nearly grown. A few years earlier Crockett had sold the cabin near the Obion and had bought another not far from the headwaters of this river, nearer the settlements. There seemed no reason why he should not leave a self-reliant woman like Elizabeth Crockett with the younger children.

On October 31, 1835, Crockett wrote to one of his brothers: "I am on the eve of starting to the Texes—on tomorrow morning. Myself, Abner Burgin, and Lindsy K. Tinkle, and our nephew William Patton from the lower country—this will make our Company. We will go through Arkinsaw and I want to explore the Texes well before I return."

Crockett took a little boat down the Obion, then walked through the forest to Mill's Point on the Mississippi, where he could board a steamer. Perhaps the others of whom he had written were with him at the time; perhaps they met him at the village on the waterfront. It is possible, even probable, that Crockett did not leave Tennessee on November 1st as he expected, but he certainly left some time early in November. During the long journey to Texas he was sometimes seen alone, sometimes with a company of men. Occasionally he vanishes from view. Little is known of the companions whom he mentioned in the letter. William Patton was in Texas when Crockett was there, but at that time he was not traveling with Crockett.

Now as throughout his life Crockett aroused talk. Stories were told of his later adventures in abundance. Some of these cannot have been true; others have the steady look of reality and are borne out by surrounding circumstance. All have a lively color, so that it is possible to see what Crockett saw, to discover many of the people whom he met, and to follow the main tracery of his movements on this rash and strange, comical and tragical journey.

9

TO TEXAS

IN EARLY November Halley's comet streamed through the sky, and almost at once snow began to fall. Great storms quickly moved southward, even into Tennessee. A bitter winter followed that for many years was called the Winter of the Big Snow. Before the heaviest snowfall, freak tempests blew on the Mississippi.

The little steamer started out at dawn, by which Crockett traveled, and he sat quietly astern through most of the trip. In his coonskin cap with the tail hanging down behind, his hunting shirt, and Betsey at his side, he looked like many another hunter of the West, and was hardly noticed.

On board were traveling Englishmen who were as quiet as Crockett. There were men with showy waistcoats, ruffled shirts, and studs of shiny glass as big as hickory nuts. There was a trader who looked as sharp as a steel trap and bright as a pewter button. Women floated by in fine furs and flowered bombazines. Within the cabin could be heard the shout of laughter and the quiet call of men at cards. Occasionally a fancily dressed tall young Negro sauntered by, the body-man of some rich planter. Below, were other Negroes going down the river.

The Mississippi stretched wide as an inland sea, yellow and gray under lowering clouds, with low dark fringes of trees on the distant shore. Suddenly a great thundergust twisted the cottonwoods along the eastern side as though they were rushes and lightning streaked into the water. A long keel boat laden with lumber spun about like a top. The river grew white, boiling in great circles, hissing and rising as rain poured down. The gayly painted little steamer bumped and heaved and rolled; men and women scurried into the cabin; there were shrieks, and anxious faces appeared at the windows.

The river began to smooth out, to grow yellow again, except for the white of treacherous riffles and chutes. It still looked, what the riverboatmen had called it, "the wicked river."

Here and there the steamer stopped to take on wood. Whenever a landing was made two great black towers of smoke shot from its smokestacks and all the people in the settlement turned out.

"Otherwise, along the river," Crockett said to an old riverboatman, "that smoke lays back small and close as a wildcat's ears."

At the mouth of the White River the waters of the open channel showed pale green where they poured into the yellow Mississippi. Inland a line of palisades marked its banks at an abrupt angle. "It's crooked," said a deckhand. "All the rivers of Arkansaw is crooked."

The White River was passed, and there were more slow hours, with the brightly dressed men and women once more on deck. Lowering clouds crept over again. The wide waters spread out and narrowed as the pilot skilfully ran through a cut-off. The shores looked far away as the steamer came out into the full sweep of the river; then the shoreline grew sharp and near, before rain fell once more.

At first sight, as the steamer reached the mouth of the Arkansas, this river with its flood of red waters seemed broad and majestic. It had rolled down from regions far to the west, joined by many branches and forks, and flowing with a broad sweep into the great valley of the Mississippi. Then, erratic and venturesome, after channeling out a new bed it often turned and made another. In one place, taking a new course, it had suddenly cut a crosswise channel back to one of its old beds, long since left dry; then for a few miles it ran in a direction opposite to that which it had been taking.

"You can expect anything from a river that'll turn around and run backward," said the deckhand.

Piloting was a perilous affair up the Arkansas.

After many hours the steamer drew up with a whistle and a clang and the usual two black towers of smoke before the cluster of huts and cabins that made the village of Little Rock. All the village turned out, and Crockett, as he passed through the small crowd, was sharply scrutinized. He went at once to the tavern, where the keeper plied him with questions, perhaps because he recognized something familiar in this face and the tall figure, perhaps only because the country was infested by robbers and every stranger was under suspicion. No doubt Crockett gave his name.

That night at supper he saw a good many men armed with bowie knives. "The Arkansas toothpick," said one of them, laying his knife at the side of his plate.

It was to be claimed in later years that the famous bowie knife was first made in Louisiana, but most stories have given Arkansas as the country of its origin. Whether the knife was invented by one of the Bowies or by an old and skillful blacksmith is not known. The original knives were of steel as finely tempered as that of Damascus. Their temper was so perfect and James Bowie was so strong that once in a small trade between himself and another man when the consideration was half a dollar, Bowie had laid a silver dollar on a plank where he split it in two with a blow of his knife. Whether or not one of the Bowies first had fashioned the knife, it was the brothers, particularly James Bowie, who had made it known through use in desperate encounters along the Mississippi and in the new territory of Arkansas.

Little was said at supper. Crockett, it seems, was in no

mood for talk. The wrench of leaving home had been deep the disappointments of the past months bitter. In the evening a strolling player gave a puppet show, and he drifted in to see it. A fiddler played while Harlequin, the puppet, performed on the slack rope, turning somersaults from one end to the other. Punch followed with his tricks, bending and snapping, then Judy in a red hat with her broom. The audience was in a roar at the quick antics of the little figures.

Crockett remained in the dusky background out of the light of the flaring oil lamps, but he had been noticed and talked about by many in the little crowd. During his career in Washington broadside sheets showing his picture had been circulated in the West, so it was hardly strange when at last one man nudged another and said, "I believe that's Crockett." A whisper went around that it *was* Crockett, and when the puppet show was ended and the songs were over a small delegation waited on Colonel Crockett in the bar of the tavern and expressed a wish to give a dinner in his honor.

A fat bear cub was hanging in the tavern shed, with haunches of venison and some wild turkeys. "They're big as ostriches," said the tavern keeper. There was small game in abundance. The next afternoon before the feast the talk ran to marksmanship. One of the Arkansawyers had sent eleven shots at long range into so small a space that it could be covered by half a dollar. Someone cried, "We told him he was good as Crockett!" At the wish of the crowd a shooting match was held, and Crockett displayed his famous skill, shooting at longer and longer range and at last twice puncturing a silver dollar in the same place. Afterwards a story was told that Crockett had punctured the dollar and then by a trick had inserted a second bullet in the same hole. The story even in Crockett's time was old and had been told of many others. Crockett was too skillful with the rifle to make such a trick necessary.

During the supper stories were told of bears in Arkansas, and the company pressed Crockett to remain and hunt with them. "The bear season is generally all the year round," observed one of the men, "and the hunts take place about as regular. Somewhere in history I read that bears have their fat season and their lean season, but that is not the case in Arkansaw where they feed on the natural productions of the soil, which is so rich that our bears have one continued fat season."

Another told of a great unhuntable bear whose marks on the sassafras trees were eight inches above those of any bear ever seen. Someone else pointed to a great turkey on the table that weighed perhaps forty pounds, saying, "Where else would you see a turkey like that except in Arkansaw? Arkansaw is the finishing up country, sir, a state where the soil runs down to the very center of the earth and the government gives you a title to every inch of it. Then, our air —just breathe *our air,* and you will snort like a horse! It's a state without a fault, sir!"

A Hoosier was present. "Except the mosquitoes," he said.

"Well, stranger, mosquitoes are nature, and I never find

fault with nature. If they are large, Arkansaw is large, her varmints are large, her trees are large, her rivers are large, and a small mosquito would be of no more use in Arkansaw than preaching in a canebrake."

Crockett matched bear stories with the hunters of Arkansas for a while, and some of them began to tell stories of the robber Murrell and his gang. One man claimed that Murrell had committed a fearsome crime not many miles away only a few nights before. Another denied this, and said that Murrell had been caught and hanged. Crockett told them that he had been brought to justice in Tennessee and added that Murrell was a quiet, pleasant-spoken man. The company was polite, but plainly doubtful.

The talk turned to less controversial questions, and grew livelier and livelier. Thirteen toasts were drunk. "You'd better stay and hunt bear," said the men crowding around Crockett when the celebration was over. "Stay and hunt, Colonel!"

"No, I'm going to Texas," said Crockett seriously. "Come you, those who can—with me. There's something happening in Texas that makes me feel I must be there. You know my motto, 'Be always sure you're right, then go ahead.' Well, I know it's right. But if I could rest anywhere it would be in Arkansaw, where the men are of the real half-horse, half-alligator breed such as grow nowhere else on the face of the universal earth but just around the backbone of North America."

News of Crockett's arrival spread rapidly; hundreds of people from roundabout flocked to see "the real critter himself." In the hospitable fashion of the country his new friends insisted upon lending him a horse, and a company set out with him for the first fifty miles of his journey. He was traveling southwest to Fulton, on the Red River.

With clearing weather, in the midst of new friends, Crockett's spirits rose. They cantered along at a good gait, still talking, telling stories, exchanging experiences that had befallen them at one time or another. The country was new, and for Crockett, as for most frontiersmen, the sight of new country was a stirring affair. Though the roads and trails were rough, the land was rich. It was still sparsely settled, with an occasional little cabin set among cotton-woods.

As the party approached the Ouachita River they suddenly heard thin strains of "Hail, Columbia, Happy Land" played on the fiddle.

"That's fine," said Crockett.

"Fine as silk and a little finer," said one of the men.

"But hark! the tune's changed," said Crockett.

Sure enough, the mysterious fiddler had struck up the tune of "Over the River to Charley."

"That's mighty mysterious," said one of the men.

"Can't cypher it out," said another.

"Let's go ahead," said Crockett, and they pushed forward rapidly.

As they drew near the river the brisk music came more and more clearly. The fiddle seemed to speak words of the song—

Over the river to feed my sheep
And over the river to Charley,
Over the river to feed my sheep
On buckwheat cakes and barley.

Crockett knew the song well and had often danced to it. When the party reached the crossing they saw an old man with a long white beard seated in a sulky in the middle of the river, playing a fiddle for all he was worth. The river was very high. The water was well over the haunches and forequarters of his thin old horse. The flimsy sulky looked as though it would be swept away any moment by the current.

"You've missed the ford," said one of the men.

"I know it," said the fiddler.

"If you go ten feet farther you'll be drowned."

"That I know too."

"Turn back," said the man.

"I can't."

"Then how'll you get out?"

"Don't know," said the old man without anxiety.

Crockett rode out to the sulky, succeeded in turning the horse, and brought the old man in his shaky vehicle safely to shore. He was a parson, and he offered to preach a sermon in return for the rescue. The company quickly declined. He said he had been fiddling to the fishes for an hour or more, and had played all his tunes, and wondered what would happen next.

Many a parson was a fiddler in these days, and there were

many such odd characters on the western roads, bent on going from here to yonder.

"In times of peril," said the parson, "I always fiddle, because there is nothing in universal nature so well calculated to draw a crowd together as the sound of a fiddler's tune. I might shout myself hoarse and nobody would stir a peg."

Crockett and his friends tightened the sulky and rubbed down the lean old horse. It turned out that the parson was also going toward Fulton, so when the men from Little Rock had pointed out the ford and had said farewell, the two started out together. When they had crossed the river the old man wound his reins around the whipstock, let his horse jog, and fiddled along the road with Crockett riding at his side. He played old frolic tunes and play-party tunes, and Crockett, who could never resist the call of a tune, was singing the words lustily at the top of his voice before he knew it. The two rode on for many miles, the old man fiddling and Crockett singing. Near Fulton the fiddling parson stopped, to turn away into the back country toward the Ozark Mountains.

"Many thanks for your good tunes," said Crockett.

"Farewell, and good luck, Davy Crockett," said the old man.

Crockett rode on into the town, in far better trim than when he had started. He quickly found a man who knew his friends from Little Rock, and they promised to see that the horse was returned.

At Fulton Crockett consorted with many men, seeking

out information as to affairs in Texas, and still keeping
in view his purpose to take up new land for a home. Some
ten or fifteen years earlier a few highly venturesome settlers had moved west of Fulton many miles into a fertile
region lying between the Red River and the Sulphur Fork.
This region belonged to Texas, but at the time the Arkansawyers thought that it belonged to Arkansas. Before going
farther south Crockett determined to explore this wild but
highly promising territory. He bought a horse and set out,
following a trail along the north side of the crooked courses
of the Red River—red from the soil—until he came to Fort
Towson, then fording in order to reach the little settlement
of Clarksville.

On the way Crockett sought out John Stiles, a famous
frontiersman of this region whom Crockett may have known
in Tennessee. Perhaps Stiles tried to dissuade him from
continuing into almost unbroken country, through which
hostile Indians were known to wander. He must have
warned Crockett of the possible dangers, but Crockett and
his party went on, passing Clarksville. Learning that he was
headed toward the wilds, a frontierswoman of great courage
and enterprise, Mrs. Caroline Clark, saddled her horse, rode
after him, and persuaded him to return to the settlement
to wait until she could find someone to act as a guide.

In later years Mrs. Clark, who became Mrs. Gordon,
often spoke of Crockett and created a picture of him that
bears the print of her own positive character. "Crockett
was dressed like a gentleman and not as a backwoodsman.
He did wear a coonskin cap. It has always disgusted me to

read these accounts of Crockett that characterize him as an ignorant backwoodsman. Neither in dress, conversation, nor bearing could he have created the impression that he was ignorant or uncouth. He was a man of wide, practical information, and was dignified and entertaining. He was a gentleman all over."

Exaggerated tales of Crockett's rudeness of bearing and appearance in Texas were told in later years; some of these pictured him as covered with skins of wild beasts, like a savage. It was these which Mrs. Clark resented. Probably he carried ordinary clothing in a carpet bag and sometimes wore it. Most accounts giving glimpses of him on this journey portray him in hunting garb; the coonskin hunting cap seems invariably to have been on his head. Probably he was not unwilling to look the part for which he was famous, that of a hunter of the West.

As to the frontier character Mrs. Clark would have been a capital judge. A woman of wit, talent, and great resource, a Kentuckian of good family, she had come to northeastern Texas in 1824 and had seen many men on that wild new boundary. She possessed an exuberance that could have matched Crockett's own. During these early years she thought nothing of riding forty miles or more to a frolic, dancing all night and returning home the next day. She danced until she was past eighty, and then was said to be "one of the sprightliest dancers on the floor."

At Mrs. Clark's suggestion two or three men had come forward to act as guides, and the next day the party set out, following scant trails to the west and hunting bear

THE NEXT DAY THE PARTY SET OUT

and turkey on the way. They seem to have been leisurely; stories have come down from old settlers of the region which portray Crockett as stopping to hunt with whoever asked him to do so. The party spent a night at the cabin of a lone settler, and Crockett busied himself making a "lizard" or "spider," a simple backwoods device of wood contrived for hauling water when pails were scarce. This he left behind for his host.

When the party had passed the headwaters of the Trinidad River they pushed on to a point now called Honey Grove, that was thick with bees and bee-trees. Crockett is said to have given the place its name. He then turned toward the Bois d'Arc Creek and Choctaw Bayou on the Red River, looking toward the territory granted the Choctaw and Chickasaw nations.

Crockett is said to have visited certain Indian tribes in Texas, and it may be that he now crossed the Red River and rode northward. Not all of his movements can be accounted for. Between the time when he is known to have been in Little Rock, about November 12th, and his arrival in Nacogdoches on January 5th, an interval of nearly two months occurred; somewhere along the way he lingered, or he took a farther journey of which no positive trace remains. His interest in the fate of the Indian tribes had been deep. Already many Choctaws, Creeks, and Cherokees had been dislodged from their former homes and were on the new lands of the Indian territory. Crockett's concern with political affairs was by no means dead, even if he had declared that he would never again seek office. Political curiosity might have spurred him to visit the Indians.

In any event his inclination to settle in this untouched, fertile region would have been strengthened by the fact that Chickasaws—who were to arrive later—and Choctaws would again be his hunting neighbors. Certainly he considered settling there. A few weeks later he wrote to his son and daughter that this was "the richest country in the world." He had found good mill streams, clear water, fine timber, and best of all, plenty of game. Hunting would offer new sport here, for herds of buffalo passed that way.

When he had explored the Red River country Crockett had planned to ride on southward through Texas to the settlements of San Augustine and Nacogdoches. His guides tried to dissuade him. The great area which he wanted to cross was threaded only by the obscure Trammell's Trace and by Indian trails. Anyone who traveled there would be in danger of attack. Tehuanas, Wacos, Ketchies, Delawares, Kickapoos, Shawnees, Caddos, were scattered over this region, most of them hostile to the whites, many of them warring upon each other. But Crockett seems to have been attracted by the dangerous prospect. He insisted upon proceeding, and the party pushed southward until they came to a great thicket, known as Jarnegan's Thicket, which would have been impassible even on foot. Faced with the thicket, Crockett at last abandoned the proposal, and returned to the Red River and finally to Fulton.

Either on the way to Fulton or later on a short trip, he spent the night in a nearby village, hardly more than a cluster of cabins, called Lost Prairie. He was short of funds. Falling into talk with a settler, Isaac Jones, he stated his predicament and offered to sell his gold watch; his name was inscribed in the cover. Jones knew well enough who Crockett was. When the deal was concluded Crockett received the man's silver watch and thirty dollars, and he promised to claim his own some day. Here he seems to have been with other travelers, but Jones spoke of him as riding somewhat apart from them.

At Fulton Crockett may have paused for a short time; undoubtedly he met there men whom he knew. Fulton was a crossroads of travel; the village was constantly thronged. Trails from the country to the west and northwest joined there with the road from Little Rock. Steamers plying the Red River from the lower Mississippi and New Orleans halted at Fulton. During Crockett's travels in the past few years his acquaintance had become greatly extended, and many Tennesseeans had settled in this region. He could hardly have failed to meet old friends.

Perhaps it was at Fulton that he assembled the sixteen or seventeen men who were to be known as "Crockett's Company." But the band may have been formed at Natchitoches, farther down the Red, in Louisiana. Some of its members may have joined Crockett on his way from Tennessee or on his jaunt into northeast Texas—for companionship, or to make a group who would settle in Texas as neighbors. Most of them came from Tennessee; records of their brief stay in Texas show that they were professional men for the most part—lawyers, doctors, engineers. Whatever their original purpose in traveling to Texas there could be no doubt as to their present decisions. Rumors of a Mexican advance were now flying thick, and they ardently joined in the prospect of defense.

Whether with some of these men or others, Crockett took passage on one of the small Red River steamers late in December or at the beginning of January.

The Red was like the Arkansas, crooked as an unwound topstring, twisting with points and sharp bends, here and there widening into swampy lakes or bayous. Often it divided into branches that a few miles farther on would reunite. Its red waters were high now, and turbid, and the steamer was so small that Crockett could stand with his feet on the lower deck and with his head upstairs. He could sit in the after-cabin and still be near the bow. He must have felt like a giant and may easily have wondered if the boat could carry him to Natchitoches.

For these small boats the machinery was tremendous. What looked like two large kettles were set firmly in brick and attached to a complicated-looking engine like a coffee mill, with two small steampipes and a big one. The big pipe smoked black smoke and the little ones let off steam. A tremendous bell would ring for departure, big enough for a cathedral, swinging to and fro twenty times or more. The big pipe would let off an extra tower of black smoke made by lighting a pitch pine knot down below. The engineer then opened the doors of the coffee mill, piled on wood, and opened all the stop cocks. A low, spiteful sizzling followed. The steampipe hissed as though it would explode, and the boat would be off, going ahead furiously. These little boats had been known to overhaul a few rafts and flat-boats by a single sudden movement and nearly shake them to pieces by the high waves they left in their wake. Making a sudden turn around a point or bend they might shave the edge of a skiff. The captains seem to have been stout, pompous men who delivered their orders in voices of thunder. When Crockett or the other tall men of his company moved on deck the boat would careen a little, and the anxious, pompous captain might call out, "Trim the boat!"

The little steamer kept plowing along with great velocity through the ruddy water, hitting banks and brushing overhanging trees with its pipes. Ahead lay red and swampy bayous with blue-black cypresses lining their shores. Often it slowed up to take on wood from immense woodpiles along the bank. Once when one of these steamers stopped for wood, a man ashore, looking it over, said the crew could come and fill their hats with chips if they wanted to. The steamer gave an angry whistle and plunged on and scraped around another bend.

"Why," said a passenger, "there's places where this river is so winding that a boat can take wood from one end of a pile in the morning and then travel all day and take it on again at night from the other end of the same pile."

Toward night something was likely to go wrong in the midst of this maneuvering. The coffee pot would give a weak sigh and be still. The captain would remark angrily that the boat would proceed the next day. At noon the steamer might be ready to start again, and would begin its familiar course, puffing and darting round bends.

Dinner was served on board, and the steward would ring a huge bell for dinner and ring it longer than any other steward would have done, and the table would reveal the largest platters of roast beef, the largest potatoes, and the largest carving knife and the largest spoons in the West.

At last the boat would warp its way to the landing in Natchitoches. But occasionally the coffee mill would explode along the way and the fussy little boat would go up in flames.

No such mishap is recorded of Crockett's journey. There is a tradition in Natchitoches that he and his friends remained there for a few days; they must have purchased horses. It cannot have been long before they were proceeding westward to the Texas border, on the way to San Augustine and Nacogdoches.

According to an Indian legend about Natchitoches and Nacogdoches a great chief of this region had once bade two of his sons travel, one to the east, one to the west. After a certain distance each was to pause and establish a village. The one who went east halted at a place that was given the Indian name of Natchitoches, on the Red River. The one who went west came to Naña, and built the village of Nacogdoches. It was sometimes said that Natchitoches meant "papaw eaters" and Nacogdoches "persimmon eaters." Both may also mean "chinquapin eaters." Chinquapin trees flourished hereabouts, with many semitropical fruits.

This was a wide, soft, opulent land, little inhabited. The soil was rich red, watered by many clear streams, and smoothly rolling. A great forest stretched before the travelers, beneath which lay a thick bright carpet of luxuriant grass. The forest was almost without undergrowth, showing open sunny spaces. Through it passed the old Camino Real, or King's Highway, of Spanish days, now only a mule trail or common wagon road, broken or lost in many places. At times the company was guided by blazes on trees. Crockett and his company camped on the way. They must have made a jovial party, for wherever Crockett was gay times followed; and these men had much in common because of their adventures along the way, and because of their abounding hopes for the future.

Plenty of game was to be had, and after seventy-five miles of easy riding they came to the little post of San Augustine. They seem to have paused there for only a few hours, perhaps for the night, but the arrival of Crockett made a stir. Cannon were fired off in his honor.

The party soon pressed on, riding many miles through the unbroken forest to Nacogdoches. A flag was flying from the top of a high liberty pole as they approached this village. Drums were beating, fifes playing. The neat little town had been established as a post and a mission by the Spanish early in the eighteenth century. It looked gay with its white houses, lying in a dell between two forks of the Naña, surrounded by wooded bluffs of some eminence. Friendly Indians were moving about. A banquet was being held in honor of Don Augustine Viesca and Don Irala, who had been officers in the Texan government, whose future was now at stake. These men had been imprisoned in Mexico, had made their escape, and were now being received with great warmth by the Texans.

When it became known that Crockett and his companions had arrived a committee was quickly sent out to bring them to the banquet. Again cannon were fired in Crockett's honor, and the townspeople poured out of their houses to see him. He made known his purpose to join the revolutionary forces, and when the banquet was ended he took the oath of allegiance to Texas, swearing to give his support to the provisional government or to any future government that might thereafter be declared.

He scanned the written oath before writing his signature, and asked to have the word "republican" inserted, so that the final phrase read "I will bear true allegiance to any future republican government that may hereafter be declared." The day was January 5, 1836.

Crockett was now a Texan. Four days later he had returned to San Augustine. Once more he was given the heartiest welcome. A ball was held, and long afterward one of the ladies told of dancing with Crockett.

From San Augustine he wrote with great exuberance to two of his children. The letter was dated January 9, 1836:

"MY DEAR SON AND DAUGHTER:

"This is the first time I have had opportunity to write to you with convenience. I am now blessed with excellent health, and am in high spirits. Although I have had many difficulties to encounter I have gone through safe and have

174

been received by everybody with open arms of friendship. I am hailed with a hearty welcome to this country, a dinner and a party of ladies have honored me with an invitation to participate with them both at Nacogdoches and this place; the cannon was fired here on my arrival and I must say as to what I have seen of Texas it is the garden spot of the world, the best land and the best prospects for health I ever saw is here, and I do believe it is a fortune to any man to come here; there is a world of country to settle, it is not required to pay down for your league of land; every man is entitled to his headright of 4,438 acres; they may make the money to pay it off the land.

"I expect in all probability to settle on Bodark or Choctaw Bayou of Red River, that I have no doubt is the richest country in the world, good land and plenty of timber and the best springs and good mill streams, good range, clear water, and every appearance of health, game plenty. It is in the pass where the buffalo passes from north to south and back twice a year, and bees and honey plenty. I have a great hope of getting the agency to settle that country and I would be glad to see every friend I have settle there, it would be a fortune to them all. I have taken the oath of the Government and have enrolled my name as a volunteer for six months and will set out for the Rio Grande in a few days with the Volunteers of the United States, but all Volunteers is entitled to a vote for a member of the Convention . . . [Here a few words seem to be omitted.] are to be voted for; and I have but little doubt of being elected a member to form the Constitution for this province. I am rejoiced at my fate, I had rather be in my present position than to be elected to a seat in Congress for life. I am in hopes of making a fortune for myself and family, bad as has been my prospects. I have not wrote to William but have requested John to direct him what to do. I hope you show him this letter and also your Brother John, as it is not convenient at this time for me to write to them. I hope you will all do the best you can and I will do the same. Do not be uneasy about me, I am with my friends. I must close with great respect, your affectionate father, farewell.

"DAVID CROCKETT."

A few days later Crockett was back in Nacogdoches. In another week he had gone southwest to Washington-on-the-Brazos. Perhaps he hoped to find Sam Houston there, another Tennesseean, who like Crockett had served in the Creek War. But Houston, who was now commander of the Texan forces, was in Goliad.

For three weeks or more after his arrival in Nacogdoches Crockett moved about in southeastern Texas, sometimes with a dozen men, sometimes with three or four. These men remain shadowy figures, and Crockett's own purposes are not plain. His movements appear from orders for provisions on the Texan government which he or others wrote for the "Tennessee Mounted Volunteers." He was headed for Bexar.

"Bexar!" "Bexar!" This short name for San Antonio—San Antonio de Bexar—was on many men's lips. In December a company of Texans had wrested this old Spanish town from the Mexican forces. and the news of this triumph had greatly heartened the revolutionary forces, for Bexar had been in Mexican possession for more than a hundred years. The town was considered the key to Texas. If the Mexicans regained it they could use it as a base for raids on the Texan colonies. In the hands of the Texans it could become, as was generally considered, an outpost for defense.

A great Mexican army was now expected; news of it had come from a hundred mysterious sources. It was not for nothing that Crockett's maxim was "Go ahead!" In early February with a few men—no one knows precisely how many—he set out for Bexar.

10

THE STORY OF FIVE STRANGE
COMPANIONS

BEFORE this last adventure is traced another story about
Davy Crockett must be told—a tale that has a gala
touch of light opera, yet is singularly life-like. This ap-
peared in "Col. Crockett's Exploits and Adventures in
Texas," which was published early in the summer of 1836.
The book was said to be based on a diary of his journey,

kept by Crockett. A pattern of evidence may yet be woven to prove that it had a basis in fact. In the main story Crockett often speaks as he might have spoken. Passages of his journey are lighted that otherwise remain dim. The principal adventures might have occurred. The tale was—and remains—part of the spreading Crockett legend; it is part of the Texas legend, and so must have a place in this narrative.

In this brightly colored story the shadowy companions who joined Crockett somewhere along the way to Texas take on definite character—a character belonging to the region and the time. They have far less dignity than those mentioned elsewhere as his fellow-travelers: but Crockett relished connections with all kinds of people. He would have consorted with any of these. Instead of a dozen companions there were four. Crockett was pictured as meeting the first of them on board the galloping little steamboat by which he traveled down the Red River from Fulton to Natchitoches.

Here is the story. Take it as true for a time.

When Crockett came out on deck he saw a cluster of men in the bow and heard an occasional burst of laughter. Seated on a chest was a tall lank blackleg, looking like a sea-serpent that had just crawled out of the black den of Natchez-under-the-Hill, down the Mississippi. He was amusing the passengers with his skill at thimblerig and was picking up their shillings as quickly as a hungry gobbler would pick up a pint of corn.

The thimble conjuror looked at Crockett carelessly and said, "Come, stranger, won't you take a chance?"

All this time he was passing the pea from one thimble to another. The game of course was to make someone wager a shilling that he could guess under which thimble the pea would be found. It seemed easy enough. The thimbles were arranged a few inches apart, in a triangle, with one in the middle. The audience would see the pea placed under one thimble and would guess that it was there. But as Thimble-rig lifted this thimble he would slip out the pea, then with a few passes slip it under another. The spectator would lose his shilling.

Crockett wagered drinks for the company that he could put his finger on the thimble under which the pea was concealed. As Thimblerig stopped shifting the thimbles and the pea, Crockett cried, "The pea is under the middle thimble," and with a swift motion he lifted it before the blackleg could raise a finger. Sure enough, the pea was there, but it would not have been if Thimblerig had moved first.

"Your eye is keen as a lizard's, stranger," a man who had lost a shilling said to Crockett.

"You've won the bet," said Thimblerig. "You've a sharp eye, sure enough, and I don't mind if I give you another chance."

"It would be little better than picking your pocket," said Crockett. "Anyway you've lost the wager."

"What about that ideer?" said a spectator who had lost a shilling. Thimblerig gathered up his thimbles and laughed, but his laugh was not altogether pleasant. He was obliged to stand treat for the entire crowd.

Afterwards on deck he set to work with his thimbles again and tried to banter Crockett into another wager, but Crockett would not be drawn. Talk dwindled, and the others moved away. Thimblerig was obliged to break off his conjuring for lack of customers, and with nothing better to do he told Crockett his story.

"I was brought up a gentleman," he said, "but through sad misfortunes I came down in the world and finally became an actor. It was a hard life. I was often hissed, and old oranges and eggs were often my portion as I was speaking my finest lines. The manager didn't appreciate my talents any more than the public," said Thimblerig, whimpering. "He put on a fine spectacle play one evening in a little town in Mississippi, called 'The Cataract of the Ganges.' Naturally for a play like that he had to have a procession with some eastern animals, and he could hardly do without an elephant. But where to find an elephant in Mississippi? Alligators were plentiful but there were no elephants. He made a pasteboard elephant, large as life. Looking around to find means of locomotion for the elephant he spied *me*, tall and rather gaunt, and he cast me for the rump. If it had been the forequarters," said Thimblerig with a noble air, "I might have had a speaking part or at least I could have snorted. I refused to act, as beneath my dignity and I was discharged, sir. I went to New Orleans and hired myself as a marker to a gambling table, and from there I moved on to Natchez-under-the-Hill, to bask amid magnolias and wickedness. Oh, I've been a bad man in my time," said Thimblerig boastfully, cocking his tall white hat on the back of his bushy head and shifting from one long leg to another.

In fact, Crockett thought, he had enough brass in his face to make a wash-kettle. He decided that Thimblerig could be trusted about as far as a tailor could throw a bull by the tail.

As they stood talking a tall chap came up from below who looked rough hewn, as though he had been cut out of a gum log with a broad ax—one of those chaps, Crockett decided, who are always ready for a fight or a frolic and don't care a toss of a copper which. Quickly another little lean chap came up from below, in a sailor's round jacket and a pigtail. The two looked at each other and evidently did not like what they saw. The tall man neighed like a horse, the little one crowed like a rooster. The two squared off. A fight might have started, but at the sound of crowing and neighing Thimblerig leapt high into the air and gathering up his thimbles dashed to the other end of the boat, rocking it until the rail nearly dipped water. The two fighters laughed. Thimblerig was lost to view even when the steamer reached the wharf at Natchitoches.

The one street of the village lay on the right bank of the river on low ground. "That swamp will grow forty bushels of frogs to the acre and alligators enough to fence it," said a traveler as the steamer tied up.

"It grows cotton, sir," shouted a stout red-faced man in a broad white hat. "Cotton! Cotton!" He shook with rage.

FIVE STRANGE COMPANIONS

Crockett went briskly to the tavern, for dusk had fallen. Thimblerig had made an adroit departure from the steamer and was there before him. In the light of pitchpine and candles—highly favorable to his enterprise—he was seated at a table with a little crowd, playing with his thimbles and picking up shillings.

The next morning at dawn Crockett was strolling through the village when the hush was broken by a voice singing a scrap of song. At the turn of a corner he came upon the stalwart but graceful figure of a young man in a hunting shirt, looking at the sunrise. He was sunburned as dark as mahogany except where his tilted cap showed the line of his forehead. He had a highly finished rifle in one hand, a shot pouch covered with Indian ornaments in the other, and he looked as cool as a morning in spring.

A swaggering fellow came down the street who seemed irritated by this composure. He came up and called the youth a scoundrel. The young man quickly handed his rifle and knife to Crockett and in a moment the swaggerer found himself under the spout of a neighboring pump, deluged by a downpour of icy cold water. The young man came back, claimed his knife and rifle, and asked if this were not Davy Crockett. He had seen pictures of Crockett, knew his story, and had even heard that Crockett was bound for Texas. He declared that he would like to join him.

"I know the country well," said the young man. "I am a bee-hunter, and you may find me of use in navigating the prairies."

Bees will move in a straight line on their flight to the

hive after gathering a store of honey, and the hunter must be clear of sight to follow them, and swift of foot. On the flower-strewn prairies of Texas the honey had a peculiar sweetness, but the fine wax was coveted even more. This was gathered and sold for candles. The youth, whom Crockett liked at once, would be a welcome companion. The Bee Hunter was to procure a pair of horses.

The next morning as the two stood ready to mount a whimper was heard. There stood the tall Thimblerig, his high white hat in his hand, begging to go on the journey. The Bee Hunter, who had known him in New Orleans, called him by name and said he wasn't half the blackguard he looked. Another horse was bought with the shillings Thimblerig had collected, and the three set out westward toward the Texas border, on the way to Nacogdoches.

The Bee Hunter was said to belong to a good family in New Orleans. In his youth he had quarreled with his father over a trivial matter and had taken to adventures along the border and on the Texas prairies. Later a reconciliation had been effected, but by that time the Bee Hunter was wedded to wild life and could not be persuaded to return.

As the three traveled, they talked of the coming conflict. They had heard that Bexar was to be held at any cost. When talk ran out the Bee Hunter sang, and the list of his songs was as long as a rainy Sunday. They followed the old King's Highway to Nacogdoches, and at last rode into the gay little town. When Crockett's presence was known cannon were fired in his honor. Here too the Bee Hunter met a sweetheart, Kate of Nacogdoches. But the trio, eager to be off, did not linger. When they set out for Bexar Kate came up with a pretty courtesy to Crockett, and turning to the Bee Hunter gave him a large gourd swung by a thong, for carrying water, some biscuits, and a new deerskin sack for his wax. A crowd had gathered, and Crockett made a speech.

The three had exchanged their horses for mustangs. At the start they hardly looked like dangerous warriors. Seated on a little mustang with his feet nearly touching the ground, the tall and hardy Crockett might have been a circus rider, except for his coonskin cap and hunter's garb. Thimblerig's high white Vicksburger was stuck on the side of his bushy head, and he too was tall in contrast to the small beast he was riding. The Bee Hunter with his trim costume and new deerskin sack made a fancy picture. Thimblerig swept the ground with his tall hat by way of a last salute, and the three were off with a clatter over the boundless plains of Texas.

Their route lay through a far expanse of canebrake. Twenty or thirty feet overhead the slender canes drooped and mingled, with tops fringing over the narrow trail. Light slanted in brokenly. They rode in a pale greenish twilight.

After many jogging hours they emerged from the dim forest of cane, and the prairie lay broad and brilliant before them. Three black wolves were running along, at too great a distance to shoot. Wild horses were scattered far off on the horizon. Flocks of wild turkey scurried and flew fanwise over the plain.

Sharply the green of the prairie grew denser, the sky black. Crockett and his companions pushed hastily on toward a distant grove of live oaks but the storm overtook them in great gusts. Bent forward in the white downpour the three tall figures on their little mustangs looked like skiffs in a tempest at sea, leaning against the wind. When at last they reached the grove the night had thickened. They found a wide dry patch under the bending branches of a live oak; their fire lighted up the leaves and boughs above them, making a great rosy dome. Lightning flashes still broke the blackness outside, revealing the wide prairie. Other groves in the far distance, with rolling verdure, and small streams, would come into view for an instant, then vanish again into gloom.

They were away the next morning in bright sunlight and rode for two days, fording small rivers and streams, shooting prairie chickens and jack rabbits for food, camping at night. When they had crossed the Trinidad River they came at nightfall to a hut where an old woman lived alone. They could not be sure whether she was Indian or white, Mexican or American; she had little to say, but she offered them shelter for the night.

Within an hour two other travelers appeared, armed with hunting knives and rifles. One was about sixty years old, tall and raw boned, with fierce black whiskers, coal black hair, a deep scar across his forehead and another across the back of his right hand. He wore a scarlet handkerchief tied around his head and a sailor's round jacket. "Seems all made up for a pirate," said Crockett to the Bee Hunter as they drew near. After a little conversation the stranger remarked that he was a pirate, and that he had sailed the main with the wicked Lafitte, whose lair had been on an island off the shore of Texas. He did not explain why he was now cruising the prairies, but he talked pleasantly enough and declared that he was on his way to join the American forces at Bexar. He seemed tired. His companion was an old Indian, stumpy in appearance, with little to say. To what tribe he belonged no one ever knew.

The Indian drew a brace of fat rabbits from his bag and some eggs of wildfowl, and a good meal was soon set on the table. But Thimblerig, who had audibly sniffed when the Pirate had announced his profession, was now giving himself lofty airs. He declined to sit down. Plainly he thought these travelers were not his equals. Perhaps he considered himself a more accomplished impostor than the Pirate.

"Stranger, I think you'd better take supper with us," said the Pirate in a mild tone. Thimblerig remained aloof. The Pirate drew his long hunting knife from his belt and laid it on the table. "You'd better take supper with us," he repeated still more mildly. Thimblerig eyed the knife, then the Pirate's fierce whiskers. He sat down. The Pirate instantly picked up his knife and cut up his meat with it.

The next morning the five started out, the Pirate and the Indian trudging along on foot at a distance. They had promised to keep the others in view.

When Crockett and his companions stopped at noon to refresh their horses beneath a cluster of trees Thimblerig took out his thimbles and began slipping the pea from one thimble to another with as much earnestness as if he had a crowd around him and a dozen shillings at stake. "Have to practice," he muttered.

All at once the Bee Hunter sprang to his feet, looked about for a moment, leapt on his mustang and without a word was off at full speed to the northeast in the general direction from which they had come, riding faster and faster, it seemed, gradually growing diminutive in size until he seemed no larger than a squirrel, and finally disappearing in the distance.

"He's gone back," said Thimblerig mournfully.

"Maybe it's a bee," said Crockett.

The Bee Hunter was hardly lost to sight when a noise arose like the rumbling of far thunder. The sky above was clear, but to the south an immense black cloud showed on the horizon.

"Burn my old shoes if *I* know what it is," said Thimblerig, whimpering and gathering up his thimbles.

The cloud approached and a roaring became distinct. The two mustangs ceased to graze and cocked their ears. Crockett caught them, took off their hobbles, and brought them within the grove. Suddenly a headlong figure emerged from the distant cloud, and in another moment a vast herd of buffalo was visible with a great black bull in front, his tail straight as a javelin in the air, his head low, his stout horns projected straight before him.

As they came close to the little island of trees Crockett drew his rifle and fired. The bull roared, and stopped. The herd behind him stopped likewise, and there was a sound of sharp concussion as the animals pressed suddenly one against another. The bull stood for a few moments pawing the ground, then darted off at an angle round the grove with the herd following, sweeping along like a tornado. Crockett's bullet had had no effect. Only a shot precisely aimed at the heart could bring a buffalo down.

As the last of the herd dashed by with a furious upturn-ing of dust Crockett jumped on his mustang, clapped his spurs, and followed in their wake. He had never hunted buffalo, and he was piqued by the failure of his shot. He rode on the trail for at least two hours but the herd grad-ually became a black cloud again and merged into the horizon. Presently all sign of it vanished.

Crockett might have retraced his path to the grove by following the buffalo trail along a back-track, but he be-lieved that he knew his bearings for a quicker route. He had not ridden an hour before he realized that he was com-pletely lost. Around him was country apparently in the highest state of cultivation, spreading as far as the eye could see, melting into purple haze. Extended fields were framed by borderings of trees. They looked like the luxuriant meadows of some thrifty farmer, brilliantly green. There were groves free from underbrush with trim margins. Here and there was the white and silver glint of running water. But Crockett heard no sound of the ax, saw no sign that man had ever visited this region before. This smooth fair country was a wilderness.

Following the sun, trying to chart a course as best he could, he pushed along. If he had found a trail he would not have dared follow it, for the Bee Hunter had told him that once when he had been lost on the prairies he had accidentally struck into the path his own horse had made earlier in the day and had traveled round and round for hours before he discovered his mistake.

As he emerged from a great grove of trees Crockett passed from the rich meadow land again into the prairie, and saw before him at a short distance a drove of about a hundred horses pasturing quietly. Some were mustangs, and there were a few beautiful coursers, descendants perhaps of those Arabian steeds brought two hundred and more years earlier into the country by the Spanish. They no sooner spied Crockett's mustang than they raised their heads, whinnied, and began moving about Crockett in a circle that gradually grew smaller and smaller until they completely surrounded him.

Crockett's little mustang seemed to enjoy the attention. He playfully bit the neck of one, rubbed noses with another, kicked up his heels at a third. Crockett decided in a few moments that the little animal had had sport enough, and applied the spur. The mustang rose straight in the air on his forefeet. Crockett kept his seat but the mustang was off in a moment at full speed, his head up, his thin little mane and tail streaming, the whole drove following swiftly in his wake. Occasionally the little horse neighed as if to keep the others near him, and on they came. The prairie lay before them as far as eye could reach, a boundless race-track. Still the little horse ran at full speed. Crockett had long since lost control of him.

The mustang kept the lead over the drove for more

than half an hour, neighing now and then in triumph and derision. But he was obliged to carry Crockett's weight while his competitors were free. A fine bay that had been close behind all the way came up side by side with him; they had it, hip and thigh. At length the bay darted ahead. Presently a second horse shot by. Others began to pass, until at last even the scrubbiest little horse in the drove passed the mustang. They had almost reached the banks of a broad river, and the bay leapt into its waters. The others followed, stemming the current and climbing the opposite bank. Freshened by the plunge they dashed off over the farther plain. The mustang sank exhausted by the river bank.

Crockett loosened the saddle and rubbed him down. The little horse, completely exhausted, lay on his side, now and then heaving a deep sigh. At times he seemed hardly to breathe at all. Crockett was convinced he would not live until morning. The predicament was dangerous enough. Where were the Bee Hunter, Thimblerig, the Pirate, the Indian? How would he reach Bexar? Even if the mustang survived, Crockett was many times lost after that headlong ride. A roaming band of Indians from any one of the hostile tribes might bear down upon him at any moment. He had no way of knowing how far he had wandered toward the Indian country.

Near the river bank was a great oak that had recently been blown down, and he decided to make a place to sleep in its branches for what protection these would afford. He gave some further attention to the little horse, then turned back to the tree, took a swift step and leaped to an upper branch, and looked through an opening in the leaves to see a restless Mexican cougar half curled on a higher limb, surveying him as a nervous epicure surveys a table before taking a good dish. His eyes glittered in the shadow like great topazes, his teeth showed white, his flat head was stretched forward. As a rule the cougar will not attack a man unless hungry or cornered, but because of Crockett's swift movement and position the animal—hungry no doubt —was now at bay. He crouched to spring. Crockett's rifle lay in a crotch of the tree, placed there by habit. He seized it instantly, leveled, and fired.

In the fraction of a second the animal had moved slightly; the ball struck the top of his head and glanced off. The cougar shook his head as though nothing more than a bee had stung him. Crockett slipped down and the cougar sprang. Crockett struck at him with the butt of his rifle but the cougar wheeled quickly and sprang again. They were now on the ground. The gun was useless. Crockett let it fall and drew his knife as the cougar closed upon his left arm. The big cat let go as the knife sank into his side, but freeing himself, came back again with increased fury. Crockett tried to blind him by a blow across the eyes but the animal turned, and the blow struck his nose instead. Stepping backward, Crockett tripped on a vine and fell. The cougar was down on him and seized Crockett's thigh. At that moment, since the cougar was turned about, Crockett grasped his tail and struck at his ribs with his hunting knife. As they scuffled they reached the river and Crockett summoned all his strength to throw the big cat over the bank, but he could not free himself and the cougar dragged him to the very edge. They seemed about to go over together, but Crockett was uppermost in the tight grasp and aimed a blow at the animal's neck. The knife entered the gullet up to the handle. The cougar struggled for a few moments, grew lax, and fell dead.

"Hunting bears is child's play to this," thought Crockett. "That cat was down on me when I fell like a nighthawk on a Junebug." He was badly scratched and his leggings torn, but that was all. The cougar had probably seen Crockett from a distance as the horses dashed to the river, had prowled swiftly through the long grass and cactus, stealthily slipping into the tree to find a vantage point from which to watch.

Crockett ate one of the few biscuits left in his pouch and looked at the mustang. The gallant little horse had stopped breathing. With no very happy reflections Crockett hung his saddle in the tree, threw his blankets across some branches, and stretched himself along this rough hammock as best he could.

At daybreak he awoke, stiff and sore from the encounter with the cougar and his uncomfortable bed. As he looked about he found not even the bones of the mustang or a piece of his hide in sight. Not so much as a mark showed near the place where he had lain. Crockett had heard nothing during the night. Another prowling cougar could hardly have carried the little horse away without noise, without leaving a trace. Whatever the cause of the mystery, the horse was gone. Lost on the prairie, Crockett knew that his danger was now more than doubled, and the biscuit had been a thin breakfast.

As he sat by the river bank trying to make a decision he saw a familiar sign in the sky far in the distance, a dark wedge that came nearer and nearer, widening. He crouched down under the cover of the fallen tree and watched until the flock of wild geese suddenly dipped toward the river, some alighting on each side. He shot a fine gander, and the flock was off, soaring high in sudden flight, honking, flapping, again pointed northward in a long wedge and soon gone. Stripping the gander of his feathers, he quickly had him on a spit roasting.

Crockett made a hearty meal and was preparing to depart with the sun for a guide when he heard the trampling of many horses. Walking out from the shelter of the tree, he saw a large cavalcade of Indians on horseback riding toward him full tilt, their knives and feather head-dresses and scarlet paint glittering in the sun. Advancing rapidly, the column divided into two semicircles and in an instant Crockett was surrounded by a hundred or more Comanches, the dreaded warriors of the plains, half naked and fully armed. The Comanches had learned of the growing strife on the Mexican border and had chosen a touch and go alliance with the Americans which might be broken at any time. They showed their sentiment to Crockett by signs and broken words. The little stream of smoke from his fire had caught their attention and they had come to investigate. When they saw the tawny body of the cougar on the river bank they were more than friendly. They saluted

Crockett as a great hunter. "Brave hunter, brave man," said the chief.

By talk and signs Crockett made known his predicament and explained that he was bound for Bexar. The chief offered him one of the spare horses and said the band would accompany him as far as the Colorado River.

Crockett rode all day with the Comanches over the prairie, in the midst of the bright glitter of their accouterments and their pleasant signs and talk. No horsemen sat more gracefully than they. Crockett was on his mettle not to disturb the reputation he had made as a hunter by an awkward turn in riding.

They had not ridden many miles before they saw a drove of horses quietly pasturing in the distance. Some of the Indians got lassos ready and darted toward them. The drove let the party approach fairly close, then with one motion started up at a canter, first circling briskly about as if to spy out what was wanted, then abruptly changing their course and running with heads outstretched, so swiftly that all but two or three soon grew small on the horizon. These were swiftly lassoed, and they reared and pawed and tore at the thongs—all but one, that made no attempt to escape but stood planted, alone and quiet, with his head down. This was a little mustang. The Indian bridled him.

When Crockett came up the rascally, scrawny, rusty little horse cast down his head and looked sheepish as if he knew what a shabby trick he had played in shamming death and stealing away in the night. It was Crockett's own mustang. One of the Comanches explained that he had been captured the more easily because he had been thoroughly broken.

Crockett rode with the Comanches all day. Toward evening they saw a small herd of buffalo in the distance and moved to a point where they could shoot, and brought down two or three. Crockett, quickly learning the art, killed a young fat heifer, and rich steaks were soon roasting over coals. The humps were sewed in a skin with the tongues and marrow bones, put into a hole in the earth, and covered with fire that would be kept burning until the following noon, when the luscious meat would be ready to eat. The Comanches were preparing a feast for their new white friend.

The sun went down as they sat at supper. The air of evening was pure and transparent. For a little while the rich green of the prairie showed against the sky.

The chief asked Crockett about the white people of his own country, and Crockett told what the Comanches would be most pleased to hear about hunting. The Comanche chief in turn told a tale of coyotes of the prairie. Crockett had learned of the Comanche song or wolf song, and asked the chief about this.

When an attack was planned it was the duty of certain warriors to move ahead of the war party at night, discover the moment for falling upon the enemy unawares, and give the signal. These warriors were called wolves, and from ancient days a song about them had come down to the tribe. As the fire died Crockett heard the chanting of the Comanches who sat in the wide circle, their wild and mournful tones rising in the blackness of the night. The tones grew deeper, but this song was not a signal for battle, and soon all was quiet.

At noon the next day the feast of juicy humps and marrow bones was held, and presently the whole band was off, riding by easy stages until they reached the Colorado River. Here Crockett might have proceeded alone, but the Comanches seemed unwilling to leave him and offered to go on until they reached a point where the Colorado crossed the old Spanish road to Bexar.

In the morning they saw a light column of smoke ascending in the clear sky from a small cluster of trees some distance away. Quickly the Indians divided in two wide semicircles, at first moving cautiously, then with a quick plunge bearing down on the little grove, surrounding it, and drawing up with a loud, raucous whoop. In the center stood Thimblerig, his brassy countenance white. He had been playing with the thimbles on the top of his white hat. His Vicksburger had now rolled to the ground, and on a bit of turf lay the thimbles and peas.

Crockett spoke. "Thimblerig is my friend," he said with a handsome gesture. The Indians gazed upon this new paleface and his queer toys with intense curiosity. Thimblerig seemed flattered by this attention and gradually regained some of his color and his swagger.

The grove was near the road to Bexar, and the Comanches pointed to the trail. Thanking the chief for his guidance and friendship, Crockett gave him a bowie knife, and the chief replied that he would always keep it for the sake of a brave hunter. Soon the Comanches were off, vanishing in a thin glittering line into the deep purple haze of the horizon.

When Crockett turned to the fire, there stood the Bee Hunter as though he had sprung out of the ground, staggering under the weight of a huge wild turkey. He had been traveling with Thimblerig, but Thimblerig had been too much occupied by his adventure with the Comanches to mention this.

When the Bee Hunter had departed so abruptly he had, as Crockett thought, spied a solitary bee taking its course toward home, and he had been unable to control his ruling passion. He had traced his tiny game through the labyrinths of the air and had found the bees many miles away in a tall oak set within a little grove. It had taken him a long time to gain his plunder, for he carried only a small ax. At first the tree had barely trembled with the sharp cracking; it was hard to fell. At last it had broken with a thundering sound, its limbs splintering and plunging into the ground, and the sun shone with splendor on the spoils of golden honey. The hollow trunk contained, as the Bee Hunter said, a "big chance of it." At least nine feet of its length was full of honey.

"There was a nation of bees," he went on, "a whole nation of bees, and they came down on me at first like Comanches on the warpath. I got stung a little, but I built a big smoky fire, and that quelled them. It seemed almost a pity to rob them of their hive when I couldn't carry the honey away. But I drained the wax and have it here in my bag. That was what took me so long. See yonder!" he cried. "There's a fine bee! He went into that tree," and the Bee

Hunter pointed to a towering oak, blue in the distance. "On a clear day, I can see a bee a mile away—easy."

Thimblerig looked at Crockett. The lid of one of Thimblerig's eyes fell upon his cheek. Crockett stared at him and said nothing.

"It's a curious fact," continued the Bee Hunter meditatively, "that bees are never found in wild country, but they always appear before the white men arrive. When the Indians see a bee, they say there comes the white man."

Then he went on with the story, with flourishes from Thimblerig. When the Bee Hunter had raced away over the prairies after his bee and Crockett had sped in a different direction in pursuit of the buffaloes, Thimblerig, left alone, had decided to retrace his steps to Nacogdoches. He expected to meet the Pirate and the Indian along the trail but he saw nothing of them. At length, however, since the Bee Hunter was returning along the track they had all first followed, the two met and decided to continue on the way to Bexar. They were almost bound to meet or overtake Crockett on the way since the Comanches were guiding him to the Spanish road.

"Well," said Thimblerig lazily, "what about a meal?" He had been eyeing the turkey with favorable glances.

"You've plucked many a traveler, you ought to know how to pluck a bird," said Crockett. "Fall to," and he looked so threatening that Thimblerig promptly went to work.

The neighing of their horses startled the trio as they were about to sit down for supper. Out on the prairie they saw two men approaching on horseback, armed with rifles. The three sprang to their feet, seizing their own weapons, for as the Bee Hunter had said, they were now more likely to meet enemies than friends. These might be Mexican scouts. But the pair turned out to be the old Pirate and his Indian companion. The Pirate explained that after they had walked a good many miles they had been fortunate enough to find a pair of mustangs hobbled in some woods.

"Couldn't say just where. They was asking to be taken. Mexican saddles," he added.

The Pirate did not tell what route he had followed with the Indian but said that he had heard somewhere along the way a rumor that Santa Anna, the Mexican general, had come out of hiding and that the Mexican forces were now no great distance from the border.

But nothing could have been less eventful than the journey of the five men for many miles. They rode through open country in which the redbud was coming toward bloom, where the grass lay like a lawn. They passed great live oaks covered with silvery Spanish moss. They rode into an arid region, covered by dwarf live oaks and twisted mesquite, then out again into green country. They saw nothing in motion except the billowing of grass in a light wind or scurrying jack rabbits and prairie chickens.

Then in the afternoon, when they were a few hours' ride from Bexar, a band of fifteen or twenty men on horseback appeared suddenly over a slight rise of ground in the distance and approached at full speed. "Look out for squalls," said the Pirate. "They're Mexicans."

"Spread and dismount and trust to our guns," said Crockett, and the five scattered in a little line, each behind his horse, Thimblerig alert with the rest.

When the Mexicans perceived this movement they checked their speed and spread their own line, then drew nearer. The leader, a tall man with a red feather in his hat, called out in Spanish. The Pirate said that he demanded surrender.

"It'll be a brush," said Crockett. "Each pick out his man for the first shot."

The Mexicans shouted again.

"Fire and be damned," said the Pirate at the top of his voice.

The Mexicans discharged their muskets but their aim happened to be poor. Crockett and his companions fired at the same moment and when the smoke rose some of the Mexican horses were seen running riderless, the leader and two others lay quiet on the ground. The remainder of the party swept away in rapid retreat. Crockett and his friends tried to follow them but the Mexicans had the start. Their horses seemed to be fresh, and they were soon lost to view.

The five companions turned toward Bexar. At last, after dusk, they saw the low outlines of the little town spread along the banks of the San Antonio. Dim lights shone out. With Crockett at their head the small band entered and was received with shouts of welcome.

As the story continues, the Bee Hunter, Thimblerig, the Pirate, the Indian, showed a noble courage at the great siege of the Alamo, and Thimblerig's bravery was touched with his usual bravado. When the Mexicans were scouting in the town of Bexar he sat on the walls and played with the thimbles, and afterward took pot-shots at the enemy from this highly exposed position. The old Pirate trudged off on a dangerous mission to Goliad, and the Bee Hunter went out in the dusk in the midst of the hot fire of the enemy to help save him on the return journey. They all died bravely. Thimblerig stayed with Crockett to the last.

These four are figures in a story; they remain as part of a legend. Yet threads of circumstance draw them toward reality. Among the defenders of the Alamo were many such obscure men; some of these had come to Bexar in groups of three or four, as volunteers. An early muster gave the name of Daniel Jackson, a sailor. At Natchitoches the Bee Hunter has been identified in tradition with a man named Johnson; and a young man named Johnson is known to have acted as a courier from Bexar to Goliad during the siege. A famous gambler of the day may perhaps be identified with the figure of Thimblerig—Jonathan Harrington Green, who was well known at Mill's Point, where Crockett left Tennessee, and in Little Rock, in Fulton, the upper Red River country, and on many western riverboats. He was traveling in Arkansas when Crockett was; he afterwards referred to Crockett as though he had known him, and spoke of events of this time as a participant. A gambler is said to have been one of Crockett's company when he entered Texas.

On this long and fateful journey, in those obscure weeks

when he was away from Nacogdoches, Crockett may have engaged in exploits not unlike those related in the story. These exploits, as they are told, were drawn from tales of the time about many men, but none is incredible; any one of them might have belonged to Crockett; they are consistent with his powers and with his character. And those wild beautiful rides over open country in the oncoming spring—on the way to Bexar Crockett must have known something equally fresh and exhilarating. In the end he must have approached Bexar much as he does in the story, to meet a hearty welcome.

11

THE ALAMO

THE SMALL town of Bexar was now almost as solitary on the great plains of Texas as the first mission had been a century before, when the Spanish fathers came, bringing their faith to wandering tribes of Indians. A hundred miles or more to the east was the small village of Goliad. Perhaps seventy miles to the southeast was Gonzales. Each was held by small numbers of Texans. There were a few settlements on the Gulf and on the Brazos River. Here and there over the wide spaces farmers' cabins had been built. The rest was open empty country. Now even the small farms and plantations clustering about Bexar were for the most part deserted.

The rumors that Crockett and others had heard on the way to Nacogdoches were true. An army of two thousand men had reached the Rio Grande under the command of Santa Anna, the Mexican dictator. A larger number had been equipped and was moving by forced marches to join them.

After wresting Bexar from the Mexicans in the early winter the Texan forces had scattered. Only a small number remained in the town, about one hundred and forty-five men. James Bowie, in command, was noted for his strength and agility as well as for his prowess with the famous bowie-knife. It was said that he could rope and tie alligators. He had come into Texas searching for great tracts of rich farm land. He had also been looking for fabled silver mines which had drawn many adventurers into the Southwest from the days of the Spanish *conquistadores* onward. A tall, fair, quiet man, with slender supple hands, he hardly looked as though he had engaged in the desperate clashes attributed to him.

William Travis, at Bexar with a company, had played a part in many encounters along the Texas border. He was ambitious, passionate, with a capacity for swift action and a great gift with words.

Many of the men were hunters from Kentucky and Tennessee; Crockett undoubtedly knew some of them, besides those in his company. He was promptly offered a command by Travis, but he refused this, saying that he preferred to remain a private. He had always been a lone hunter, and he maintained this position until toward the end, though there seems to have been an understanding that the men from Tennessee should stand together.

From the first there had been small clashes of authority, jealousies, and uncertainties at Bexar. The place had been stripped of supplies; Houston had sent Bowie there from Goliad about the middle of January with orders to have the town abandoned; he was certain that sufficient forces could not be mustered to defend it. But Bowie, on arriving, had decided otherwise, and wrote, "We had rather die in these ditches than give it up to the enemy." Travis, courageous to the point of rashness, probably wanted the command held by Bowie. There was constant friction between the two men, and this may have been deepened by other forces whose direction cannot be fully traced. Beneath all the exultant movement of the new settlers in Texas were swift political undercurrents. Since the outbreak of the Texas Revolution it had been difficult to maintain a clear policy among men who were widely scattered, whose interests were diverse. Houston, in general command, was not yet secure in that position.

Perhaps the rankling of an old anger and the force of settled conviction had caused Crockett to throw in his lot with Bowie and Travis. Houston was a sworn friend of Jackson's, and partisanship as to the Jacksonian policies had reached into Texas.

The strange circumstance was that these three men, with

different purposes, should have clung to their position at Bexar. The magnet that held them there seemed to hold the volunteers as well. For the most part they had come to this new land as Crockett had come: because distances spoke to them, because they liked unpremeditated adventure, for land—a handful out of many in those days who flung themselves against heavy odds and took hardy enterprises easily. In the face of oncoming danger they determined to hold Bexar because it was a last outpost, a key to Texas; enthusiasm for a free Texas was running high. They were governed by another motive, mighty if intangible. Frontiersmen were accustomed to hold what they had taken, then move onward. In the glowing future which Crockett saw so plainly—of which he had written with such warmth to his children—Bexar would become only one of a succession of settlements, stretching farther and farther into the West. A whole people was resistlessly moving, claiming new land, often quickly leaving it, pressing onward, "ahead!" They gave many reasons for their eagerness, but their reasons were not so good as their courage, not so clear as the power that drew them to untouched country.

In spite of differences in authority these obscure days of mid-February at Bexar must have been full of suppressed triumph, glittering purposes, gay talk. Crockett was popular with all the men; he made speeches, told stories. Never a fiddler, he apparently found an old instrument somewhere in the town and amused the company by his efforts to play. Sometimes he joined in rousing competition against a Scotsman's bagpipes, lifting his voice in song against the lusty medley. News from east of the Mississippi was to be traded. Headrights to land were surely discussed. There must have been tales of the warring tribes of Indians to the north, and of trappers who had gone into the Rockies and beyond. There was warm gossip of men and events along the border, much laughter, many jokes, much drinking. If the talk turned to Mexican advance there could have been only one shout, "Let 'em come!"

Suddenly, silently, the Mexicans in Bexar fled from the town. Within a few days it was clear that the Mexican army was approaching at last.

The story goes that one evening something that might have been a pile of leaves was seen to move in a distant patch of chaparral where the ground was gray and dry. Presently a figure stood up, ran, and drew near a cluster of men on the edge of the town. It was a hunter who had been absent from Bexar for several days on a scouting expedition. His jacket and leggings were so gray and tattered that he could easily have lain down again against a hillock and have been taken for part of it. Indians to the south had told him that the Mexican army was now nearing Bexar, planning their first great attack there. The shout went up, "Let 'em come!"

"I'm a whole menagerie, Colonel," the hunter told Crockett after delivering his news, "shaggy as a bear, wolfish about the head, stealthy as a cougar on the hunt. I've heard you could grin till the bark'll peel off a gum log. So can I. Let 'em come!"

A more substantial account is that scouts were sent to

discover whether the Mexicans were proceeding toward Bexar, as had been reported in the town. A party went out and from a rise of ground could discern the great army drawn up for parade, with the officers moving up and down, gesticulating.

As a signal to the people of Bexar the bells of the church of San Fernando were rung; and the defending forces moved into the fortified mission of the Alamo, about half a mile from the town. A stoutly built granary adjoined it, with a baptistry and other small rooms. From the northwest corner of the church a wall twelve feet high extended for fifty feet to the long barracks, a two story building. From the southwest corner a strongly built stockade ran for seventy-five feet to the low barracks. The buildings and walled enclosures covered about two acres of ground. Cannon had been mounted on the scaffold of the church and on the barrier walls. The stockades and walls were thick. But at least a thousand men were needed to defend the Alamo.

Santa Anna arrived at the Medina River with his army on the night of February 20th. The next morning the dark line of the Mexican forces was seen in advance. Provisions at Bexar were short. Travis hastily sent out a scouting force which brought in eighty or ninety bushels of corn and twenty or thirty beeves.

Bowie suddenly became helplessly ill. The command passed to Travis. Within a few days Travis became sick. According to one story—flying no one knows from where—Travis, realizing his condition, begged Crockett to assume command of the forces in the coming struggle. Crockett declined, but there was no question as to the eagerness of his service. In one of his many letters Travis wrote that "Colonel Crockett was seen at all points, animating the men to do their duty." Crockett offered to go on a dangerous errand to Goliad, but Travis evidently preferred to have him remain at the Alamo.

Within a day or two the great Mexican army was seen approaching Bexar in solid regular formation, their officers on brightly decked horses. They entered the town and took possession. The next morning a messenger was sent by Santa Anna to Travis, demanding unconditional surrender and declaring that he would put every man to the sword in case of refusal. The only answer from the Alamo was a cannon shot. In counter reply the Mexicans ran up a blood red flag to show that they would give no quarter. They then bombarded the Alamo for twenty-four hours from a distance. So thick were its walls, so securely were it defenders entrenched that not one was lost. The fortress seemed as solid at the end of the bombardment as before. The Mexicans, weary from their long forced marches, did not press the siege. But those within the mission can have had no sense of security; to a man they must have known their peril.

The night of February 24th Travis despatched Colonel Bonham to Goliad, bearing a letter that has been called the most heroic document in American history. It was addressed "To the People of Texas & All Americans in the World."

"FELLOW CITIZENS AND COMPATRIOTS, I am besieged by a thousand or more of the Mexicans under Santa Anna. I have sustained a continual Bombardment for 24 hours & have not lost a man. The enemy has demanded a surrender at discretion, otherwise, the garrison are to be put to the sword if the fort is taken. I have answered the demand with a cannon shot & our flag still waves proudly from the walls. *I shall never surrender or retreat*. Then, I call upon you in the name of Liberty, of patriotism & everything dear to the American character, to come to our aid with all despatch. The enemy is receiving reënforcements daily & will no doubt increase to three or four thousand in four or five days. If this call is neglected, I am determined to sustain myself as long as possible and die like a soldier who never forgets what is due to his own honor & that of his country.

"VICTORY OR DEATH.

"W. Barrett Travis,
"*Lt. Col. Comdt.*"

At the same time Travis sent a volunteer who knew the land to go east to Gonzales for assistance there. At the most fortunate nothing could be expected from any of these expeditions for several days.

The Mexicans rested, awaiting reënforcements, contenting themselves with intermittent firing. Within the Alamo there was the restless waiting of men who were compelled to remain inactive, who would gladly have faced their fate at once. Fresh Mexican contingents were arriving.

At the end of six days, in the gray dark of the earliest dawn, thirty-two volunteers crept into the Alamo. They had come from Gonzales. They were all cheerful, though they knew well what the outcome would be if the Alamo were lost. There was still no word from Bonham. Another messenger had been sent to follow him. Thinking that both might have been captured by a Mexican contingent, Travis sent another volunteer to carry word to Goliad.

The same evening when dark had fallen Travis sent still another messenger bearing a letter to the village of Washington-on-the-Brazos, where Texans were writing a Declaration of Independence:

"The spirits of my men are still high, although they have had much to depress them. We have contended for ten days against an enemy whose number are variously estimated at from fifteen hundred to six thousand men. . . . Col. Fannin is said to be on the march to this place with reënforcements but I fear it is not true, as I have *repeatedly* sent to him for aid without receiving any. . . . I look to the colonies alone for aid; unless it arrives soon I shall have to fight the enemy on his own terms. I will, however, do the best I can under the circumstances; and I feel confident that the determined valor and desperate courage, heretofore exhibited by my men, will not fail them in the last struggle; and although they may be sacrificed to the vengeance of a Gothic enemy, the victory will cost the enemy so dear, that it will be worse for him than defeat. I hope your honorable body will hasten reënforcements, ammunitions, and provisions to our aid as soon as possible. We have provisions for twenty days for the men we have. Our supply of ammunition is limited. At least five hundred pound of cannon powder, and two hundred rounds of six, twelve and eighteen pound balls, ten kegs of rifle powder and a supply of lead, should be sent to the place without delay under a sufficient guard.

"If these things are promptly sent and larger reënforcements are hastened to this frontier, this neighborhood will be the great and decisive ground. The power of Santa Anna is to be met here or in the colonies; we had better meet it here than to suffer a war of devastation to rage in our settlements. A blood red banner waves from the church in Bexar and in the camp above us, in token that the war is one of vengeance against rebels; they have declared us as such; demanded that we should surrender at discretion, or that this garrison should be put to the sword. Their threats have no influence on me or my men, but to make all fight with desperation and that high-souled courage which characterizes the patriot who is willing to die in defense of his country's liberty and his own honor."

During the night the Mexicans had established two batteries on the farther side of the river and had posted a company there. Cavalry was sent to occupy the eastern boundaries beyond the town and the trail toward Gonzales. Clearly the enemy was attempting to surround the Alamo, but on two sides lay open country cut by ditches that the defenders could easily command.

Provisions in the garrison grew still more meager. Bowie became critically ill. The next morning heavy cannonading began; bombs were thrown into the stockades. These exploded without mischief. Another day passed, of tension, expectancy.

Before dawn on the following morning Bonham returned. There was no hope of assistance from Goliad. Colonel Fannin had assembled three hundred men with cannon, other arms, and ammunition, and had started out with a wagon train for Bexar, on receiving Travis's message. But the expedition had been too hastily improvised. The wagons with their heavy loads had broken down on the rough trail and the scant provisions had given out. It was impossible to cross the swollen rivers and streams with the artillery. Fannin with his men had been obliged to turn back, and as they did so word came that another contingent of the Mexican army was marching on Goliad. He was compelled to retain his forces for the protection of the people of Goliad. Fannin had urged Bonham to remain in Goliad, since he was certain either to be intercepted by the enemy or to fight against overwhelming forces at Bexar. Bonham had said, "I will report to Travis," and had started back at once on the hazardous journey, making his way by night, stealthily evading the enemy who were now widely posted over the prairie. A few hours later the second messenger who had gone to Goliad slipped in. He too had declined to remain there.

There were cheers when Travis said that if the enemy took the Alamo his men could only fight to the last gasp, making conquest mean the heaviest possible loss to the victors. Even as they cheered, shells began to fall about the fort with increasing frequency, now from shorter range. Though not in command Crockett was everywhere at once with the swiftness of the hunter of the forest, taking shot after shot over the parapets, hastening below to reënforce the doors still further, mustering more men to take positions above and hurrying there again to use his own sure aim.

The defenders remained at their posts all day with shells flying into their midst; not one of them was lost. They picked off Mexican gunners from a distance. They shot warily into the chaparral, catching the enemy as they dodged from low hillock to hillock or crept near the fort from buildings within the town. Toward nightfall the Mexican forces had succeeded in maintaining positions nearer the Alamo, making a partial ring just out of gunshot.

At midnight Travis had his cot carried into the nave of the church and summoned the entire garrison before him. The Mexican bombardment had not begun. Travis's words echoed in the dim stillness.

"We are overwhelmed," he said, "and our fate is sealed. Within a few days, perhaps within a few hours, we must be in eternity. It is no longer a question of how we may save our lives, but how best to prepare for death and serve our country. If we surrender we shall be shot without taking the life of a single one of our enemy. If we try to make our escape we shall be butchered before we can dispatch our adversaries. To either of these courses I am opposed, and I ask you to withstand the advance of the enemy. When they shall storm the fort and scale our walls at last, let us slay them as they come. As they leap over the ramparts, slay we all of them until our arms are powerless to lift our swords in defense of ourselves, our comrades, our country. Yet to every man I give permission to surrender or attempt to escape. My desire and decision is to remain in the fort and fight as long as breath remains in my body. Do as you think best, each of you. Those who consent to remain with me to the end will give me joy unspeakable."

Weak as he was Travis raised himself from his pallet,

stood, and stepped forward. With his sword he drew a line across the floor. He called upon the men to take their position.

"Those who will remain and fight until we die, step across this line to my right."

Crockett was the first to step forward. At the same moment James Bowie, who was still sick, called upon his friends to carry his bed across the line and place it beside Travis. Every man in the garrison walked across the line except one, who covered his face with his hands.

"You seem unwilling to die with us," said Travis.

"I am not prepared to die, and shall not if I can help it," he answered. "I speak the language of the enemy fluently. Perhaps I can get through the lines."

No one interfered with his departure. Nothing further was ever heard of him. It has been denied, with good evidence, that even this one man left.

What Crockett thought during these moments none can guess. Perhaps he remembered rivers and forests he had known well. Perhaps he thought of his children and of his wife. Since he was given to action he may have thought most of the desperate work that lay ahead.

At least five thousand of the enemy were now assembled. During the night of March the fifth Santa Anna quietly prepared a great assault upon the mission. In silence four storming columns took their places, provided with ladders, crowbars, axes. With the hooves of their horses muffled, cavalrymen seized strategic points around the town to cut off the possibility of escape or reënforcement. Sharpshooters ceased their sniping in the chaparral, the artillery was still. The thick ring about the Alamo was now complete. Men were posted at every vantage point in the houses and on the streets.

As the first glitter of light fell upon the river and the town a bugle was sounded by the Mexicans, and the assault began. Afterwards Santa Anna insisted that he would have surprised the garrison had not one of the columns raised a shout as the bugle sounded: but the men within the Alamo had been expecting such an attack and were at their posts as the solid masses of the enemy pressed forward with the rat-tat-tat of drums. Guns roared from the streets. Shells rained over the parapets of the fortress, faster, nearer.

On the walls the defenders—Crockett among them—picked off cavalry leaders and those infantrymen who were rolling cannon forward. But the enemy pushed over the dead bodies of their comrades, advancing, narrowing the space between themselves and the fort. Their numbers were overwhelming. Their ranks, now blurred by clouds of smoke, moved still nearer. As many dropped under fire others crowded into their places. The ring of men, horses, cannon, smoke, grew dense. The Mexicans reached the plaza in front of the Alamo, and its walls were battered with rams and cannon. Soldiers swarmed over the ruins into the monastery court, and from the north side battering rams struck against the thick walls of the church. Ladders were raised.

As the enemy climbed the ramparts they were met by the swift crack and deadly fire of rifles but as half a dozen of them fell backward to the earth others were ready to clamber into their places. The cannon on the roof no longer spoke. Fierce hand to hand fighting followed as the Mexicans climbed over the walls. Most of the Texans were quickly cut down by the overwhelming numbers. Some of them fought their way in retreat to the church below, only to find the enemy in full force there. After persistent ramming the monastery wall had given way, and the Mexicans had swept through the breach. The north door was being attacked with rams. Some of the Texans, drawing together in the nave of the church, had thrown together sacks of sand for ramparts and began shooting with nails, scraps of iron, whatever they could find with which to load their guns.

The doors of the church were now shattered by great blasts of powder, and the outer walls of some of the little rooms that opened upon the courtyard were attacked. The Texans still held the nave of the church but they were now approached from three, then four, sides. Fighting inch by inch against the rain of grape and canister, inflicting a terrible carnage, a small party of the defenders reached the baptistry, which had withstood the battering rams from without and was still uninvaded. One of the men tried to blow up a powder magazine there that they might die by their own act rather than at the hand of the enemy. He failed in this, shot through the heart by a Mexican bullet as he was lighting the fuse. The Texans fought in a blaze of powder, in clouds of smoke. Their ammunition gave out, and they fought with clubs, with their bare hands.

THE ALAMO

Travis had manned a gun at the beginning of the attack and was almost instantly killed. The command was said to have passed to John Baugh, and after his death to Crockett. In the wild confusion Crockett seems to have been everywhere at once. A story was told afterward that as he leveled and fired his famous "Betsey" he sang invitingly to the Mexican, "Won't you come into my bower?" This would have been like him; perhaps he was heard singing this song in the earlier days of the siege. But when the final attack began there would have been no time for song, nor could any tune have been heard in the terrific din.

In later years it was said that five men were captured by the Mexicans at the end of the siege and that Crockett was of this number; these men were supposed to have been taken before General Santa Anna, who ordered them put to the sword. But Crockett was not taken prisoner. In the remembrance of a man like Crockett, in telling a story so heroic as that of the Alamo, the imagination of many people was touched. They evoked scenes as sharply as though they had been present, and told of them as though each episode in stories they had heard contained the entire truth. Strangely, a woman, Mrs. Dickinson, a little girl, and a Negro lad were safely concealed in one of the outer rooms; they were spared by the Mexicans, and it is in some of the tales told about them that Crockett was pictured as among the group of captives taken by General Castrillon before Santa Anna. Five Texans were captured, it is true, and slain at Santa Anna's command, but Crockett was not among that number. Mrs. Dickinson herself told the true story.

No quarter was given in battle; none was intended. Throughout the assault the Mexicans played the diabolical *degüello,* meaning "no mercy," an ancient battle-tune played by the Spanish centuries before in their wars against the Moors. Crockett fell in the thickest of the swift and desperate clash. Travis had asked him to defend the wall on the south side toward the barracks; it was here that the fighting was hottest. The men from Tennessee fought with him. He fell with them, fighting bitterly. Mrs. Dickinson spoke afterward of seeing him lying among the slain, with his fur hunting cap at his side.

For twelve days the small garrison of Texans had withstood an army that had increased to numbers thirty times its size. The final assault was over within an hour. All the defenders were gone, none remained to tell the whole history. "Thermopylæ had its messenger of defeat, the Alamo had none."

All were lost, but their final end in that lonely place had something of barbaric glory. A huge pyre was built with cords of wood, and the bodies of the defenders were destroyed by great towering flames near the charred, broken walls of the Alamo. Spring was coming in abundance. The acacia was golden. Blue buffalo clover would flower fresh as rain, lying in sheets of deep azure like water showing the southern sky. Along the creeks and water-courses the red-bud and wild plum were feathered white and purple red.

The harsh struggle was not ended by this great disaster.

"REMEMBER THE ALAMO! REMEMBER THE ALAMO!"

The wide, empty land was still a prize. Other battles swiftly followed between the Mexican and the Texan forces, at Goliad, at small places farther south along the Gulf. "Remember the Alamo! Remember the Alamo!" became the Texan battle cry. The Republic of Texas was declared, and Sam Houston directed the scattered forces. Triumph came at last under Houston. Santa Anna, with all his great army, was forced to sue for peace. The end of the conflict was ten years distant when the Americans sought both to hold Texas and to gain California, and the issue was fought in the Mexican War.

"Remember the Alamo! Remember the Alamo!" Even in those later years the words became a rallying cry. Songs were made about Crockett. One of these would have pleased him, for it was sung to an old and lively frolic tune called "Gray Goose."

> Remember gallant Crockett's bones
> Have found a glorious bed there.
> Then tell them in your thunder tones
> No tyrants' feet shall tread there.
> Come gather east, come gather west,
> Come round with Yankee thunder,
> Break down the power of Mexico
> And tread her tyrants under.

It was an odd circumstance that the tune "Gray Goose" should have been linked with Crockett's name, for the gray goose had been an emblem in his family.

In the reign of Louis the Fourteenth of France a handsome youth was for a time a member of the court, named

Antoine Desasure Perronnette de Crocketagne. He became a Huguenot. When the Huguenots were expelled from France he went to England with his young wife, then to Ireland, and changed his name to Crockett. He took for his crest the wild gray goose, noted for the altitude of its flight, its grace of motion, its power of wing, and for the fact that it flies against the wind.

Other Crocketts went from France to England and to Scotland, and the arms of the English family also showed wild birds, three crows, with a motto that Davy himself might have chosen, "Crow not, croak not." The arms of the Scottish Crocketts showed words that a frontiersman might have spoken, "Let sleeping dogs lie."

But it was the Irish family that formed the ancestral line of Davy Crockett. The son of the handsome Huguenot married a girl from Donegal. His son in turn married a Huguenot who had come to Ireland, and these two emigrated to Virginia. They were Davy Crockett's great-great-grandparents. The fate was a strange one that could lead a single family in successive generations from the gayest court in the world to the early frontier of the West, then farther and farther into wild land, and finally into one of the great battles of history, on a far frontier. In one way or another they had all flown against the wind. The gray goose with its great power of wing was a fitting emblem for Davy Crockett.

12

SUNRISE IN HIS POCKET

A FEW men had gathered about the fire in a tavern on the Forked Deer River in western Tennessee. The winter dusk had fallen. An old hunter was speaking, mournfully.

"Thar's a great rejoicing among the bears of the river country and the alligators of the Mississippi are rolling up their shining ribs to the sun. The rattlesnakes has been coming out of their holes this autumn to frolic in the clearings, and the foxes goes to sleep in the goose pens. It's because the rifle of Crockett is silent forever, and the print of his moccasins is found no more in our woods."

"The painters and bears will miss him," said another hunter.

"He never missed *them*," said a man with red hair who was bending over the barrel of a flintlock, oiling it.

"I heard Davy never died at all," said a hunter.

"I heard he was a roaming over the prairies of Texas with a bear," said a traveler.

"Named Death Hug," said the red-haired man.

"He was carrying messages for Sam Houston," said the traveler, "and he was stopped by a big party of Mexican scouts. Quick as lightning Crockett mounted Death Hug and leapt clean over their heads." There was a pause. "Another time when he was carrying those messages he met a squad of Mexicans just as he came up to a grove of oaks and Death Hug ran right up one of the oaks with Crockett on his back and then out on a limb as slick as a panther going to roost, and over to the limb of another oak, and another, and then they were down and away."

"And once he sighted a stallion on the prairie," said the old hunter, "wild as the whirlwind, and tall and strong. Crockett came within a hundred yards of him, and the stallion threw back his ears, spread his jaws, and came snorting at him. As the horse reared to plunge Crockett seized his mane and mounted him as easy as a cow bird sits on the back of a brindle bull. The stallion made off like lightning and a big thunderstorm came up. Lightning struck all around but it flashed to either side of the horse as he ran and never struck him. The horse was off to the west and Crockett thought he was going to be flung against

226

the Rocky Mountains. He ran for three days and three nights until he came to the Mad River, that poured down the mountainside boiling and hissing. There the horse ran under a tree, trying to brush Crockett off his back, but Crockett pulled his mane and that stallion leapt over the tree and the boiling river besides. Then he stopped quiet and Crockett got off."

For twenty years after his death stories were told of Davy Crockett as though he were still alive. It was said that he had been shot by a silver bullet that had made no wound and left no trace, and that he had feigned death at the Alamo, and had concealed himself when the battle was over. Then—in the story—he had set out to avenge the death of the five prisoners whom the Mexicans had put to the sword. He had found the slayers and had killed them with his hunting knife. Afterwards he was seen on the prairies far to the north, hunting buffalo.

"Sometimes Crockett rides wild horses, sometimes he rides Bear Hug when he goes hunting buffalo," said the traveler. "Once he got trace of two mammoth buffaloes from the wilds of Oregon that snorted blue fire and bellowed small thunder. When they got in a particular passion they used to butt trees down and bore a hole in the earth twenty feet deep before they could cool off their dispositions. Crockett put off to the spot where they were and found them just as the hurricane of their temper was up and they were snorting young lightning and roaring bass music and had uprooted a few trees and tossed them into the air for practice. They were going to play toss with Crockett too, but he slipped round and tied their tails fast together, got between them with their tails like traces and with each of his arms over their flanks drove them a hundred miles, and they were as tame as sucking sheep."

He went on: "Another buffalo was so big and noisy and kept up such a continual thunderstorm of roaring that he used to scare away the sunrise, and the prairies was dark for days, but Crockett shot him on the wing and invited some Comanche warriors to the feast. It was night, and as they were making ready a great light appeared on the horizon. The light came nearer and nearer, and it was a prairie fire with billows of smoke and flame a foaming and a tossing in the air like waves at sea and a roaring like the sea. It came nearer and nearer to where Crockett was with the Comanches, as if it were going to sweep right over them, but a breeze came up and the fire swayed away a little. The breeze got to be a great wind and the fire turned and went off in another direction. Away went Davy after it with all those buffalo steaks in his hands holding them out in front of him and he kept on going until the steaks was well roasted. Then he came back to the Comanches and they had their feast."

"They was one buffalo Crockett captured out on the prairies and he tamed him," said the man with red hair, "and he called him Mississippi. When Crockett came to one of those border towns Mississippi was with him, and Mississippi would go to meeting every Sunday morning. He sang the bass of 'Old Hundred,' never missing a note, and that same critter would even lend the leader his horn for a tuning fork!"

"It's a caution what will happen in those border towns out on the wild prair*ee*."

It was not only hunters of the Great Valley who told stories about Crockett. Trappers from the far west said that they had seen him in the mountains of California, hunting grizzlies. Sailors back from long voyages in the South Seas declared that he was there, hunting pearls.

"Out there in the South Seas he was a diving," said a sailor, "and he came to a cave. He crawled till he came to dry land under the deepest water of the ocean. It was dark, so he made a lampwick out of his hair and soaked it with elbow grease and made a light by striking his knuckles on a rock.

"Crockett looked around and discovered that he had got in among thousands and thousands of pearl oysters that were fast asleep in their beds. He sang a song and danced a measure or two, and the oysters woke up. They all opened their shells for him and he came ashore with sacks and sacks of pearls."

Someone repeated this story in a stage coach that was traveling slowly at night in western Kentucky. The light in the coach was dim, showing the dark figures of men in every seat.

Other tales about Crockett were told as the coach rumbled, the wheels creaked, and the hooves of the horses thudded against hard clay first at a walk, then at a trot, then at a walk again.

"I understand," said a man in a tall beaver hat, "I understand that Crockett has not lingered in the Far East but has returned to the great prairies of North America to hunt the buffalo, the deer, and the elk. Only the other day I learned that he had crossed the Cannon Ball River and was following the crooked courses of the Missouri."

"I am credibly informed that Davy Crockett has now reached the Mississippi," said a small man with an air of importance. "In fact a friend of mine who has a dwelling on its banks witnessed a curious adventure of his. Crockett was out hunting one day when he noticed a wing-broken goose riding on the surface of the river. He struck out after it. You know that Davy Crockett can swim faster, dive deeper, stay down longer, and come out dryer than any man in all creation. Just as he was about to seize the goose a loud howl rose suddenly near him. Crockett jumped up out of the water like a sturgeon. It was a wolf, only a few feet away. At the same moment an alligator swam toward him from another direction and from overhead the whole flock of wild geese flew down upon him, hissing and flapping their wings.

"Davy dove down slantwise so as to come up far beyond the reach of all these critters, but when he struck the bottom of the river he was chased by a river calf and had to swim straight up to the surface again. The wolf, the alligator, the geese, were still there and the river calf was hot foot after him besides! Crockett struck out for a sawyer and just then a little steamboat came whistling and tooting along with fire and black smoke, and scared all the critters away. Crockett asked for a passage on board. Death Hug came along at this moment, swimming in easy water, and Crockett requested a berth for him too. The captain was a fussy man and he refused to give a berth to Death Hug, so Crockett and his tame bear walked out of the water and into the woods where they cut down a very ancient hollow gum tree, hewed it open on one side with Crockett's knife, corked up both ends, and launched their canoe into the river just as the steamer got out of sight. Old Death Hug sat in the stern and steered with his tail. He lit a pipe and so did Crockett. Death Hug paddled with his paws and Crockett with his hands. Smoking like smokestacks, they made that hollow log canoe walk in and out and along the water until the fishes stared, and soon they passed the steamboat. After a while Death Hug wanted to go ashore, so the canoe was drawn up on a bank. Crockett took a log for a pillow and floated downstream, and was soon fast asleep.

"I suppose you gentlemen have heard what happened to him next," queried the little man as though he hoped they had not.

From the darkest corner of the coach a traveler spoke up. "I reckon it's just about there he met up with Ben Hardin!"

Now a certain Ben Hardin was a member of Congress from Kentucky, an orator, and a good deal of a humorist. Ben Hardin in the stories was a different figure altogether. Many tales were told of the frolics and adventures of Crockett and this curious personage in the Shakes and on the Mississippi—"the backbone of North America"—where Crockett had once traveled with his staves. These stories are full of wind, earthquakes, hurricanes, lightning. Not all of them could have been related in a single evening, no matter how long the journey.

Here are a few of them, set down as they were told in the talk of the day.

As Davy Crockett was drifting downstream, asleep on his log pillow, he was wakened by bumping into something. Before him was a strange equipage for river travel. In the center of a log three kegs had been fastened one on top of another, and on the topmost keg was sitting a fat little man wearing a snug tarpaulin hat that looked as bright as a new dollar. His trousers were of sailcloth, his shoes thin and light with ribbons on them. He wore a big black patch over one eye.

"Well, stranger," said Crockett, "you must have robbed a peddler and got off with all his flashy trumpery."

"Why," said the fat little man, "the critter's got the lingo of a Christian. I thought I had spoke to a catfish. I've plowed salt water for forty year and I've seen porpoises and dolphins and mermaids, and I've took many a Nantucket sleighride, but you're the queerest looking sea craft I ever come across, on soundings or off. Where you cruising, old rusty bottom?"

The little man's voice grew deeper and rougher as he spoke. He had a voice so rough it couldn't be written down but would have to be shown in a picture.

"You infernal heathen," said Crockett, "I suppose you're new down this way, but I'll tell you I'm a snorter by birth and education, and if you don't go floating along and leave me to finish my nap I'll give you a taste of my breed, beginning with the snapping turtle!"

At this rejoinder the fat little stranger looked as mad as a shovel full of hot coals. He took a string of tobacco out of his pocket and bit into it savagely. He bit off a string long and big enough to hang a buffalo with, and roared out, "I'll shiver your mizzen, you landlubber! You rock crab! You deck sweeper!"

Crockett's steam was up. "I'll double you up like a spare shirt. My name is Crockett—"

With this the stranger roared with laughter, and his laugh was as rough and noisy as his talk. Stooping down he reached out his hand. "Give us your flipper. I wouldn't hurt a hair of your head for all the world. I've been cruising up and down this river a looking for you. Hurrah for Davy Crockett!"

The stranger explained that his name was Ben Hardin and that he was a man who had seen great times. "My business is seeing," he said jovially, and added that he had been told he could see more with the black patch over one eye than any other man could see with it off. He said he had been captain of ships that had turned bottom upward and sailed along to their destinations on their masts. He said that he had leaned his back against a hurricane. He said that he drank bitters made out of whiskey and rusty cannon balls, and slept coiled up like a cable. The last time he counted he was going on into his ninety-ninth year.

As Hardin was talking a noise was heard like low thunder, then a distant roaring like the voice of old Niagara.

"Hello," said Crockett, "there's a storm coming."

"No, it's a steamer," said Ben Hardin.

"Maybe it's the echo of our voices," said Crockett.

The noise grew louder, the water began to squirm about, and Crockett's log and Hardin's little craft began playing see-saw. Then came a sudden roaring blast that would have made Niagara sound like a kitten. The trees on shore walked out by the roots and danced about. Houses came apart. Two boats on the river crashed into each other, and their ribs were stove in to the boilers. Crockett and Hardin thought it was time to be off.

When a streak of lightning glanced by, Crockett seized it by the fork and sprang upon it. For a man who had leaned his back against a hurricane Ben seemed in a hurry to leave. He gave a leap and seized Crockett's hair. Crockett greased the lightning with some rattlesnake oil he happened to have along and the way they left the tornado behind and slid across the land was astonishing to all nature.

When this feat became known people talked about greased lightning. They still do. "Quick as greased lightning."

When this adventure was over Crockett landed with his new friend in the woods, and he felt as good-natured as a soaped eel. He invited Hardin to come along to his cabin, where he promised him a bear steak, and the two went along through the woods as good friends as a tame hawk and a blind rooster.

But the way Ben walked was a caution, for he was used to the decks of a ship. When it came to walking among the tall masts of the backwoods he turned every way but the right way. He swung about like a bearskin hung to the limb of a tree.

One morning Ben wanted to go out hunting. So out they went and away went Ben, whistling and swinging his tarpaulin hat at every little creature that happened to be in sight. At last they got under an oak that was famous for breeding many generations of wildcats. Even its knots looked like wildcats' eyes. Just as they got beneath it and were going to take a seat on a root they heard something above them give a scratch and a grunt. Ben ran up the tree as light as a monkey up a ship's ladder. He hadn't gone further than heels out of sight when Crockett heard a sailor's regular rough language with all the trimmings. He looked up and saw a bear, and the creature had grabbed Ben by the shoulder. The way the old sea serpent fought back was a caution. Down they came to the ground, Ben and the bear, and rolled over and over. The leaves began to turn claret color so Crockett stepped up, squeezed the breath out of the bear, and gave Ben a swallow out of the lightning bottle. Ben swore that every claw of that bear was a whaler's harpoon.

Ben Hardin told Crockett that he was a whole squall and a hurricane at a frolic. Old sailors used to say that he could dance all the girls in all the seaports from Cadiz to Cape Cod out of their stockings. He danced till he wore away the stone steps in front of Crockett's cabin.

"Well, old Salt-Rope," said Crockett, "I'll give you a frolic that'll last you for a seven years' cruise."

Now Ben had said that Crockett's daughter was as pretty as a dolphin. "I've seen dolphins and mermaids too," he added. The story was that she had once been captured by Indians who carried her away and tied her to a tree, and meant to kindle a fire about her. But while they were gone for wood, panthers came and gnawed the ropes and set her free, and gathered about her as she ran through the forest and escorted her most of the way home.

"Anyway she's the true grit," said Crockett, "and she can dance anything from an earthquake reel to a square-toed double trouble shiver."

They all went to the Asphaltum Flats where lightning couldn't strike because the Flats were so hard. An old man with a hemlock fiddle played new tunes that went so fast a humming-bird's wing couldn't keep time with them. Crockett set Ben and the girl at it, and away they went, and the Asphaltum Flats looked like a prairie on fire. "After the first three tunes," Crockett said, "Old Ben began to grunt like a saw going through a pine knot. Then he staggered. My girl said nothing but kept on leading out every new tune. After the hundred and fifteenth tune Ben began to roll like a ship in a sea-storm and finally he fell over and curled up in his pigtail. But my girl was ready to go on."

Strange tales were told of Crockett's hunting exploits in wild country of the Northwest and of his encounters with

Indians. One evening about dark Crockett and Hardin came to the great Indian Rock, which was the hardest stone in all creation.

"It was so 'tarnal high and so all flinty hard," said Crockett, "that it would turn off a common ordinary every-day streak of lightning and make it point down and look flat as a cow's tail."

They got under a shelf of this great rock, and Crockett struck a little fire from it with his knuckles to light their pipes, and they began puffing. They looked up and the whole stone around and on both ends was alive and red with Indians, all with guns and tomahawks. Ben reached for his flintlock but Crockett saw that lightning would be the only thing so he rubbed himself against the shelf of the rock and struck his left eye two or three times. Then he stepped back and with a single wink sent such a blasting streak of hot lightning into the great rock that it parted into forty thousand pieces. There were red Indians shooting up into the sky like rockets and landing way out on the prairie. "We cut stick in such a shower of red Indians as was never seen before," said Crockett.

Another time Crockett and Ben Hardin were having a feast of roasted buffalo with some friendly Indians near one of their lodges. Afterwards Crockett danced a break-down on a great flat rock nearby. He rattled off some clear music as he danced and all the Indians came out and sat around in a circle to watch him—all but the Indian chief who began a regular Indian war dance in opposition. The Indians began to shout and whoop. Crockett went at it harder and danced until the old rock began to snap and smoke like a hemlock back log. Fire began to fly about, the Indian chief's feet began to singe, and the blankets of the others were all in a light blaze. Just as the Indians were all going to run off Crockett finished with a regular old "Grind the Bottle," and stamped the whole fire out again.

Farther to the north Crockett and Ben Hardin went wolf hunting. After the hunt one day when Crockett was feeling hot and lazy, the old sailor bantered him for a race on the frozen river. Now Crockett was a rocket on skates. Skating, he could pass the swiftest Indians, and Indians could go fast as thought on their bone runners made of buffalo ribs. Up and down the frozen rivers of the north Crockett would go, leaping great air holes twenty feet or more across and skating on without losing a stroke. Death Hug was also a prime skater, though not so good as Crockett. For the race Death Hug started off ahead while Davy and Ben started even. They went so fast they struck fire against the wind. Sparks flew out of the ice and made Crockett's gun go off so he lost a stroke but he skated ahead and grabbed Death Hug's tail. At the same moment Ben fell. He caught hold of the tail of Crockett's hunting shirt and down the river went the three for a hundred miles like a toboggan, with Death Hug in the lead.

Traveling over the country in winter Davy and Death Hug came to the Niagara River, which was frozen. They were cutting all sorts of frolic flourishes on the ice when suddenly the great piece on which they were skating parted from the rest and headed toward the Falls. There were people all along the banks and Crockett waved at them. Suddenly Crockett and his bear were left on only a small wedge of ice that was sharp at one end. Death Hug put his paw to his nose, Crockett raised Uncle Sam's starry handkerchief, and they steered over the great hill of water as easy as though they were on a greased ship.

Then Crockett mounted his old pet alligator and steered right back up the roaring thunder-water as slick as a stream of wind going up a chimney.

"My old alligator walked up that monstrous great hill of water as easy as a wildcat goes up a white oak," said Crockett. "And my alligator opened his mouth as wide as the Black Cave, and the people were all astonished."

On the Upper Lower Fork of the Great Little Deep Shallow River Davy gathered all his animals around him. Death Hug was there, and Mississippi, the buffalo that could sing "Old Hundred," and a cougar, a fox, a wolf, and a hyena. Crockett's pet hyena could outlaugh an earthquake, and he was so wild that the northeast wind couldn't reach him and even the lightning couldn't catch up with him.

"The lightning put out after him once," said Davy, "but he laughed it out of countenance and ran away, and when I followed him I had to run for seven days and seven nights. Then he turned round and came home with me as docile as a kitten."

Crockett gathered them all together under the Liberty Tree. It was the Fourth of July, so he took out his bag of patriotism and gave them an oration. "When I began my oration," said Crockett, "they opened their eyes and ears in the most teetotal attentive manner and showed a 'tarnal sight more respect than the members of Congress show one another during their speeches, and when I concluded by lifting my cap with twenty-six cheers for Uncle Sam and his states, with a little thrown in for Texas and Oregon, why choke me if those critters didn't follow with such a shout as set all the trees to shaking!"

Then Crockett taught all the animals the polka. Death Hug and the buffalo Mississippi and the old alligator could wear down an oak floor in a single night, all flipping their heels in regular polka step while Ben Hardin whistled the tunes. Ben could outwhistle the prettiest clarionette that ever talked music.

Stories about Crockett are still told in Kentucky and Tennessee and in the Ozark Mountains. Even now people in the Ozarks talk about him as though he were still living just over the next ridge.

They say that once he went bear hunting in the fall up on Whangdoodle Knob. At sundown he was tired out so he lay down under a big old dead cedar tree and went to sleep. In his sleep he rolled over and nearly broke his powder horn. Above him was a little curved yellow branch and he hung his horn on it. The next morning the horn was gone and he couldn't find the branch. That night he came back to the Knob and soon the little crescent moon came up, riding low over the mountain. It came so close and looked so yellow it nearly blinded him, and there was his powder horn hanging from the tip. He reached it down and went along home to his cabin.

In the Ozarks they tell of another time when Crockett was out hunting and traveled far from his cabin and spent the night in the woods. The next morning at daybreak he took a far jump and landed on the sun, thinking that he would be carried over the mountain to his cabin. But he had forgotten that he was west of his cabin instead of east. So, traveling with the sun for twenty-four hours, he saw the whole world, and dropped off the next morning and landed on his own doorstep.

During his own lifetime Crockett had been spoken of as consorting on easy terms with the moon, with shooting stars, a fiery comet, and the lightning. In all the stories his close companions were wind, water, fire, the earth, and the wild creatures of forest and prairie. In a last story he is portrayed as stronger than the sun, and he appears once more in the hunting country of Tennessee.

This story belongs to the Winter of the Big Snow, the winter of 1835, when Crockett set out for Texas, when snow fell early through the wide stretches of the North, crept farther and farther down through the hard wood forests of Michigan, then through the soft wood forests, through the long valleys of Wisconsin, down upon the prairie country of Illinois, into Kentucky and Tennessee. The story was told as if Crockett himself related it.

"On one of those winter mornings it was all screwen cold," said Crockett. "The forest trees were so stiff they couldn't shake and the very daybreak froze fast as it was trying to dawn. The tinder-box in my cabin would no more catch fire than a sunk raft at the bottom of the sea. All creation was in a fair way for freezing fast, so I thought I must strike a little fire from my fingers and travel out a few leagues and see what I could do about it. I brought my knuckles together like two thunderclouds, but the sparks froze up before I could collect 'em, so out I walked and tried to keep myself unfrozen by going along at a frolic gait, whistling the tune of 'Fire in the Mountains' and keeping going at three double quick time. Well, after I had walked about a hundred miles up Daybreak Hill I reached Peak o' Day, and there I discovered what was the matter. The earth had actually frozen fast on her axis and couldn't turn round, and the sun had got jammed between two cakes of ice under the wheels, and there he had been shining and working to get loose till he was frozen fast in his cold sweat.

" 'C-R-E-A-T-I-O-N,' thought I, 'this is the toughest sort of suspension, and it mustn't be endured—something must be done or human creation is done for!' It was so premature and antediluvian cold on top of Peak o' Day that my upper and lower teeth were all collapsed together as tight as a frozen oyster. So I took a big bear off my back that I'd picked up on my road and threw him down on the ice and soon there was hot sweet bear oil on all sides. I took and squeezed him over the earth's axis until I'd thawed it loose, and I poured about a ton of sweet bear oil over the sun's face. Then I gave the earth's cog wheel one kick backward till I got the sun free and whistled 'Push Along, Keep Moving.' In about fifteen seconds the earth gave a grunt and began to roll around easy, and the sun walked up most beautiful, saluting me with such a wind of gratitude it made me sneeze.

"I lit my pipe by the blaze of his topknot and walked home, introducing people to the fresh daylight with a piece of sunrise in my pocket."

So when Davy Crockett set out for Texas the earth was no longer screwed up stiff and frozen fast, but rolled around. The sun walked up in the morning and down at night, though the days were bitter cold and the snow lay deep.

BEHIND THIS BOOK

BEHIND THIS BOOK

CROCKETT became famous as a hunter, but he was also a farmer. The letter[1] written from Nacogdoches to his son and daughter shows him ready to embark again on the vocation that had always occupied him, this time on a vast scale. So it was fitting that numbers of the legends and tales told about him in his own day and after his death should have appeared in those small handbooks of wind and weather, the farmers' almanacs—the so-called Crockett almanacs. The first two issues of these were published in Nashville in 1835 and 1836, and the copyrights were taken out in his name. Perhaps he had a hand in the new project before he left for Texas. Later numbers of the series were issued as by the "Heirs of Col. Crockett." But since "Snag and Sawyer" and the mythical Ben Hardin or Harding were also named as publishers of early issues, the connection with Crockett and his family may only have been part of the expansive comic legend.

Whatever their origin, these almanacs at once became highly popular. The Nashville series was continued for several years, and until 1856 others were published in New York, Boston, Philadelphia, and elsewhere; there were many scattered numbers. Some fifty issues have been dis-

[1] In the possession of Mrs. T. M. Hiner of Granbury, Texas, a granddaughter of David Crockett's.

covered. The equinoxes and solstices, the risings and settings of the planets and stars and the calculations of the moon's phases were occasionally burlesqued, but for the most part they were seriously given. Almost at once the scope of the almanacs was widened to include sketches of Daniel Boone, Mike Fink, Kit Carson, the Cape Cod sea-serpent, and other great legendary figures of the day. Delicate, serious, and fairly accurate little pieces were inset on natural history in the West. But Crockett remained the dominating figure—the mythical, comical Crockett. Fragments of talk were ascribed to him that seem allied with his own talk, and may have been written down from memory. Stories were printed that he himself might have told, and perhaps had told. Many soaring inventions about his exploits found a place.

Some of the stories are borrowed from older mythologies, like that of the silver bullet. The legendary Crockett often resembles the heroic figures of established myth—leaping across great spaces and moving about readily among the planetary bodies. In the brief "Sunrise in His Pocket" he is a fire-bringer. But no effort was made to create a consistent mythology. The finer stories came out at wide intervals, in different series. "Sunrise in His Pocket" was one of the last. The alliances with the older myths seem easy and unconscious. Doubtless many frontiersmen, particularly those of Celtic origin—the Scotch and Irish who made substantial numbers in Kentucky and Tennessee—were familiar with their native myths, at least in shadowy reminiscence. Identities between the Crockett stories and Indian lore may be traced. But the tang of humor is our own; the stories are ours in shape and color and in patterns of speech. They seem to spring from wild country. Whoever first told them had seen wildcats flash through the branches of a white oak and knew the hunter's life well. Into them are woven the life and high fantasies of new frontiers.

Here and there a historian has suggested that Crockett's fame, both in his own lifetime and after his death, was created by Whig politicians, and that they evoked the legendary Crockett. But the politicians who possessed this singular imaginative power have not been identified. And the historians cannot have scanned the almanacs. Few traces of a political bias appear in these small paper volumes.

It is true that some of the stories seem to have been made to order in printers' offices. Many are as crude as woodcuts by an unpracticed hand. Some may have had their origin in printed materials about Crockett. The story of the stallion that Crockett mounted and rode through thunder and lightning to the Mad River may have been evolved from Crockett's experiences with the little mustang as related in "Col. Crockett's Exploits and Adventures in Texas." But surely it is plain that other, more primitive elements went into the making of the story of the stallion. This should be allied with contemporary tales of the white steed of the prairies and with certain Indian legends. Even so, it springs clear of obvious origins and is complete in itself. However it began, somewhere along the way it received a fresh infusion of creative energy.

The sources of this energy are not far to seek. When all possible alliances have been noted, the legendary stories about Crockett seem to have had a firm basis in popular story-telling. Their humor is of an order that was rising like a tide in the eighteen thirties, forties, and fifties. Crockett himself had given this a strong momentum. By his character, his repartee, his stories, his exploits, he had captivated the popular imagination, and his name kept this afire. These stories constitute one of the earliest and perhaps the largest of our cycles of myth, and they are part of a lineage that endures to this day, in Kentucky, Tennessee, and in the Ozark Mountains. Here they join with similar comic-heroic stories about other well-known figures.

In eastern and middle Tennessee tales that have been attached to Crockett are told interchangeably about John Sevier or Andrew Jackson. Others are attached to obscure hunters of local fame. One tale told of Crockett in the Ozarks may properly belong to Andrew Jackson, that by which Crockett rides a razor-back hog from Fayetteville to New Orleans. There is a Fayetteville in the Ozarks, but Fayetteville in Tennessee is the point from which Jackson started with his troops at the beginning of the Creek War, carrying his triumph to New Orleans. Mr. Edd Winfield Parks of Cumberland University, Lebanon, Tennessee, has discovered a number of these interchangeable stories. Mr. Wayman Hogue and Mr. Vance Randolph report Crockett tales as told in the Ozarks. The stories from the Ozarks repeated here have been drawn from Mr. Vance Randolph's "Ozark Mountain Folks" (New York, 1932).

BEHIND THIS BOOK

In the main the stories told in the final chapter of this book have been drawn from the Crockett almanacs. These have been freely used elsewhere when they have seemed consistent with Crockett's recorded speech. The small sketches of natural history in the almanacs have also been used with freedom since they were closely allied with the Crockett tales and accurately represent scenes which he knew. Publication of the Crockett almanacs stopped abruptly in 1856, and their rich legendary store has remained almost untouched.[1] The following list of these has been compiled from the outstanding collection in the library of the American Antiquarian Society, which possesses nearly every issue listed here. The substantial collection in the Library of Congress has been used for purposes of comparison, as have collections belonging to the Carnegie Library of Nashville, the Wisconsin Historical Society, and to Mr. Franklin J. Meine of Chicago. In compiling this list the writer has had the very generous collaboration of Mr. Clarence S. Brigham, Director of the American Antiquarian Society.

> Davy Crockett's Almanack, of Wild Sports of the West, and Life in the Backwoods. Calculated for all the States in the Union. Snag and Sawyer. Nashville, 1835. *Go ahead!*
> Davy Crockett's Almanack, of Wild Sports in the West, and Life in the Backwoods. Calculated

[1] Stories about Mike Fink, drawn from these almanacs, appear in "Mike Fink," by Walter Blair and Franklin J. Meine. (New York, 1933.) The Crockett almanacs also furnished materials for "American Humor," by Constance Rourke. (New York, 1931.)

for all the States in the Union. Vol. I, No. 2. Published for the Author. Nashville, 1836. *Col. Crockett's Method of Wading the Mississippi. Go ahead!*

Crockett's Yaller Flower Almanac. Go ahead! Snooks, no danger her going off! The Ringtail Roarer! Ripsnorter! Circumflustercated Grinner's Guide! Snagsville, Salt River: Published by Boon Crockett, and Squire Downing, Skunk's Misery, Down East. Elton. New York, 1836.

Davy Crockett's Almanack, of Wild Sports in the West, Life in the Backwoods, & Sketches of Texas. *O Kentucky! The Hunters of Kentucky!!* Published by the heirs of Col. Crockett. Vol I, No. 3. Nashville, 1837. *Go ahead!*

Crockett's Texas Oldmanick. Turner & Fisher. New York, Philadelphia, 1837. *"Crockett goes a-head, though dead." Millions for Texas! But not a cent for taxes!!! With comic engravings of all the principal events of Texas.*

Davy Crockett's Almanack, of Wild Sports in the West, Life in the Backwoods, Sketches of Texas, and Rows on the Mississippi. Published by the heirs of Col. Crockett. Nashville, 1838. *Go ahead!*

Crockett Comic Almanac. Vol. I, No. 2. Elton. New York, 1839. *She's a little 'un, But she's a good 'un.*

Crockett's Awlmanaxe for 1839. Turner & Fisher. New York. No. 1.

The Crockett Almanac. Containing Adventures, Exploits, Sprees, & Scrapes in the West, & Life and Manners in the Backwoods. Vol. II,

BEHIND THIS BOOK

No. 1. Published by Ben Harding. Nashville, 1839. *An Unexpected Ride on the Horns of an Elk. Go ahead!*

The Crockett Almanac, Containing Adventures, Exploits, Sprees, & Scrapes in the West, & Life and Manners in the Backwoods. Vol. II, No. 2. Published by Ben Harding. Nashville, 1840. *Crockett scared by an Owl. Go ahead!!*

Crockett's Comic Almanack. A. Skinflint. Albany, 1840.

The Crockett Almanac, Containing Adventures, Exploits, Sprees, & Scrapes in the West, & Life and Manners in the Backwoods. Vol. 2, No. 3. Published by Ben Harding. Nashville, 1841. *Tussel [sic] with a Bear. Go ahead!*

The Crockett Almanac: Containing Sprees and Scrapes in the West, Life and Manners in the Backwoods; and Exploits and Adventures on the Praries [sic]. Correct Astronomical Calculations for every part of the United States, Territories, and Canada. J. Fisher. Boston, 1841. *A Squabble in the Mud. Go ahead!*

—— Same, varied edition.

Crockett's Harrison Almanac for 1841. Elton. New York, 1841.

Ben Hardin's Crockett Almanac. With Correct Astronomical Calculations; For each State in the Union—Territories and Canada. Rows—Sprees and Scrapes in the West; Life and Manners in the Backwoods: and Terrible Adventures on the Ocean. Turner & Fisher. New York and Philadelphia, 1842. *Go Ahead!*

253

Ben Hardin's Crockett Almanac. Correct Astronomical Calculations; for each State in the Union—Territories and Canada. Rows—Sprees and Scrapes in the West: Life and Manners in the Backwoods: and Terrible Adventures on the Ocean. Turner. Baltimore, 1842. *Ben Hardin on a Raft. Go ahead!*

Crockett Comic Almanac. Worser Gotham. Published by Doleful Serious, and sold at 98 Nassau, and 18 Division Streets. New Series, No. 1. New York, 1842. *Lots of Funny Fun.*

Crockett Almanac, Improved Edition: Containing Real Stories. S. N. Dickinson. Boston, 1842.

Fisher's Crockett Almanac. Edited by Ben Hardin. Calendar for the whole Country. With Rows, Sprees, and Scrapes in the West: Life and Manners in the Backwoods: Terrible Battles and Adventures on Sea and Land. Turner & Fisher. New York, Philadelphia, 1843.

I leave this rule for others when I'm dead,
Be always sure you're right, then go ahead.

—— Same, variation in imprint.

Davy Crockett's Almanac. Life and Manners in the Backwoods: Terrible Battles and Adventures of Border Life: with Rows, Sprees, and Scrapes in the West. Turner & Fisher. New York, 1844.

Davy Crockett's Almanac. Life and Manners in the Backwoods: Terrible Battles and Adventures of Border Life: with Rows, Sprees, and

Scrapes in the West. For Eastern, Northern and Middle States. James Fisher. Boston, 1844.

> *I leave this rule for others when I'm dead,*
> *Be always sure you're right, then go ahead.*

—— Same, varied imprint.

Davy Crockett's Almanac. Calendars correct for the entire Union, the territories, Texas, and the British Provinces. James Fisher. Boston, 1845.

—— Same, varied imprint.

Davy Crockett's Almanac. Calendars correct for the entire Union, the Territories, Texas, and British Provinces. Turner & Fisher. Philadelphia, New York, 1845.

> *I leave this rule for others when I'm dead,*
> *Be always sure you're right, then go ahead.*

—— Same, varied imprint.

Crockett's Almanac. Scenes in River Life, Feats on the Lakes, Manners in the Back Woods, Adventures in Texas, &c, &c. Calendar calculations for the whole union. James Fisher. Boston, 1846.

Crockett's Almanac. Scenes in River Life, Feats on the Lakes, Manners in the Back Woods, Adventures in Texas, &c, &c. Turner and Fisher. Philadelphia, New York, 1846. *Crockett's wonderful escape up Niagara Falls, on his Pet Alligator.*

Crockett's Almanac. Scenes in River Life, Feats on the Lakes, Manners in the Back Woods, Adventures in Texas, &c, &c. Calendar calculated for the whole union. J. B. Keller. Baltimore, 1846.

Davy Crockett's Almanac: Daring Adventures in the Back Woods; Wonderful Scenes in River Life; Manners of Warfare in the West; Feats on the Prairies, in Texas & Oregon. Calendar Calculations, correct for the Whole United States. Turner & Fisher. New York, Philadelphia, 1847.

I leave this rule for others when I'm dead,
Be always sure you're right, then go ahead.

Davy Crockett's Almanac. Daring Adventures in the Back Woods; Wonderful Scenes in River Life; Manners of Warfare in the West; Feats on the Prairies, in Texas and Oregon. James Fisher. Boston, 1847.

Crockett's Almanac. Calculated for the whole United States. Turner & Fisher. Philadelphia, New York, 1848.

Crockett's Almanac. Calculated for the Whole United States. James Fisher. Boston, 1848. *The Birth of Crockett.*

I leave this rule for others when I'm dead,
Be always sure you're right, then go ahead.

Crockett Almanac. Calendar Calculated for the whole United States. Turner & Fisher. Philadelphia, New York, 1849.

Crockett Almanac. James Fisher. Boston, 1849.

Crockett's Almanac, Containing Rows, Sprees, and Scrapes in the West; Life and Manners in the Backwoods, Adventures on the Ocean, &c. Fisher & Brothers. New York, Philadelphia, Boston, 1850.

Crockett's Almanac. Containing Rows, Sprees,

and Scrapes in the West; Life and Manners in the Backwoods. Adventures on the Ocean &c. R. Magee. Philadelphia, 1850.

Crockett's Almanac—Containing Life, Manners and Adventures in the Backwoods, and Rows, Sprees, and Scrapes on the Western Waters. Fisher & Brother. Philadelphia, New York, Boston, 1851.

Crockett Almanac, containing Life, Manners, and Adventures in the Back Woods, and Rows, Sprees, and Scrapes on the Western Waters. With Handsome Illustrations. G. W. Cottrell & Co. Boston, 1852.

I leave this rule for others when I'm dead,
Be always sure you're right, then go ahead.

Crockett Almanac, Containing Life, Manners, and Adventures in the Back Woods, and Rows, Sprees, and Scrapes on the Western Waters. With Handsome Illustrations. Fisher & Brother. Philadelphia, New York, Boston, Baltimore, 1852.

Crockett Almanac, Containing Life, Manners, and Adventures in the Back Woods, and Rows, Sprees, and Scrapes on the Western Waters. Fisher & Brother. With handsome illustrations. Philadelphia, New York, Boston, Baltimore, 1853.

Crockett Almanac. Containing Life, Manners and Adventures in the Backwoods, and Rows, Sprees, and Scrapes on the Western Waters. Fisher & Brother. Philadelphia, New York, Baltimore, 1854.

Crockett Almanac. Containing Life, Manners and Adventures in the Backwoods, and Rows, Sprees, and Scrapes on the Western Waters. Philip J. Cozans. New York, 1854.

Crockett Almanac. G. W. Cottrell & Co. Boston, 1855.

Crockett Almanac. Fisher & Brother. Philadelphia, New York, Baltimore, Boston, 1855.

Crockett Almanac. Philip J. Cozans. New York, 1856.

Crockett Almanac. Fisher & Brother. Philadelphia, New York, Boston, Baltimore, 1856.

—— Same, varied imprint.

Stories, verses, and songs about Crockett appeared in many news sheets of the day, in "albums," "galaxies," and other similar compilations. On the whole these references are unimportant except as they indicate that Crockett's name was one to conjure with. Trace of a "Crockett Song Book" has been found. A small volume published about 1846 contains a number of songs about Crockett and others alluding to him:

The National Songster: Embellished with Twenty-five Splendid Engravings, Illustrative of the American Victories in Mexico. By an American Officer. New York. n. d.

Minstrel songs of the eighteen thirties and forties contained allusions to Crockett, and occasional stanzas of these or of other songs about him may still be heard in the South.

A volume called "Leisure Hour Musings in Rhyme"

(1871) has oddly been attributed to Crockett by serious writers. Later, stories about him appeared in the dime and half-dime novels or the similar weeklies, as was inevitable because of his character and career, and also because the almanacs were—among other things—precursors of that favored form of reading. Three of the dime or half-dimes in which Crockett figures may be mentioned, though they have not been used for the purposes of this book:

> The Texan Trailer, or Davy Crockett's Last Bear Hunt, by Charles E. LaSalle. Beadle's Dime Novels, No. 231.
>
> Davy Crockett's Vow; or His Last Shot for Vengeance. The Five Cent Wide Awake Library, No. 729. Frank Tousey, Publisher.
>
> Dead Game, or Davy Crockett's Double, by an Old Scout. *Pluck and Luck Weekly*. No. 412.

If the legendary Crockett has been remembered mainly in obscure places, certain essential facts as to his character and career have also drifted away. The books ascribed to him have had a curious history. Four books bearing his name were published during his lifetime or shortly after his death:

> A narrative of the life of David Crockett, of the state of Tennessee . . . Written by himself. Philadelphia, 1834.
>
> An account of Col. Crockett's tour to the North and down East, in the year of Our Lord one thousand eighteen hundred and thirty four. His object being to examine the grand manufac-

turing establishments of the country; and also to find out the condition of its literature and morals, the extent of its commerce, and the practical operation of "The Experiment." Philadelphia, 1835.

The Life of Martin Van Buren, heir-apparent to the "government," and the appointed successor of Andrew Jackson. Containing every authentic particular by which his extraordinary character has been formed. With a concise history of the events that have occasioned his unparalleled elevation; together with a review of his policy as a statesman. Philadelphia, 1835.

Col. Crockett's exploits and adventures in Texas: wherein is contained a full account of his journey from Tennessee to the Red River and Natchitoches, and thence across Texas to San Antonio; including his many hairbreadth escapes: together with a topographical, historical, and political view of Texas . . . Written by himself. The narrative brought down from the death of Col. Crockett to the battle of San Jacinto, by an eye-witness. Philadelphia, 1836.

It has been denied that Crockett wrote any or all of these books. The question is important. Here is living testimony as to the man—or something spurious, at least in part. What remains that is truly Crockett's? An answer as to the "Narrative" lies in the following:

Register of Debates in Congress. Vols. IV, V, VI, X, XI. Washington, 1827, 1828, 1829, 1830, 1834, 1835.

Address of Mr. Crockett, to the voters of the ninth district of the state of Tennessee. Washington, 1829.

Sketch of the remarks of David Crockett on the bill for the removal of the Indians, made May 19, 1830. Washington, 1830. Also *in* Speeches on the passage of the bill for the removal of the Indians, delivered in the Congress of the United States, April and May, 1830. Boston, 1830.

David Crockett's circular. To the citizens and voters of the ninth congressional district of the state of Tennessee. [Washington, 1831]

Almost surely someone gave a bit of polish to the speeches in Congress before they were recorded. The same hand may have touched up the "Address of Mr. Crockett" and the "Circular," or even the brief speech on Indian removal, though this was certainly set down in a form close to the written word. Admit the intrusion of another hand: none the less if these speeches are read against the background of current debate their highly individual flavor becomes unmistakable at once. They are eager, positive, ardent, not too well ordered; and the turn of language is close in both rhythm and tone to that of the "Narrative."

Other abundant testimony as to Crockett's natural style remains, in his letters, appearing in the collections of the Tennessee Historical Society, the Library of Congress, the New York Public Library, the New York Historical Society, the Historical Society of Pennsylvania, the Boston Public Library, the Yale University Library, the Library of

261

the University of Texas, in excerpts from printed catalogues, and in the collections of a number of private individuals. Dashed off in haste, these letters are full of quick allusions to the political situation of the moment; they contain bits of news, often with the crack of wit and a rough onslaught against Jackson and his friends. Hardly one lacks a definite friendly word for the distant correspondent. The letter accepting the invitation to a public dinner at LaGrange, Tennessee, after Crockett's final defeat, was an easy, dignified response.[1] The letter to his brother,[2] written on the eve of his own departure for Texas and full of small personal matters, was written as though nothing was more natural than for Crockett to pick up a pen.

Still another letter,[3] dated "Steam Boat Curier near Maysville, 5 May 1830," suggests his ability to sketch an episode. Traveling from Washington, he had brought with him a portrait of himself, given him by the artist. He had rolled it up in newspapers, marked it "A Map of Florida," and had tied it inside the mail stage—he was in the accommodation stage. The two stages were parted somewhere along the way, and when he changed seats he was told by the driver of the mail that the roll had already been sent ahead. When he overtook the second mail stage it was missing. He was in a great flurry. He thought a Negro might have taken it. He thought someone had not told him the truth. He sent a flying sketch of the facts to one Josiah Sprigg,

[1] From the catalogue of Thomas F. Madigan, of New York.
[2] In the possession of Mrs. Seneca D. Powell of Portland, Maine.
[3] Owned by Judge W. A. Rhea, School of Law, Southern Methodist University, Dallas.

somewhere back on the road, hoping that the portrait might be recovered, and his hasty pages are full of mood and action.

Crockett never concealed the fact that he had the manuscript of the "Narrative" "run over by a friend or so, and that some little alterations have been made in the spelling and grammar." He makes this statement in the preface. In a letter [1] to Carey and Hart, dated Washington City, February 23, 1834, he gave the name of the friend who assisted him. It is a long letter, in which he shows himself eager to see his book; he also discusses the question of the English copyright. The main portion has to do with an emphatic arrangement by which Thomas Chilton, member of the House from Kentucky, was to receive one-half the profits of the book. At the death of either Crockett or Chilton the share of each was to go to the heirs. Crockett added, "The manuscript of the Book is in his handwriting though the entire substance of it is truly my own. The aid I needed was to Classify the matter but the style was not altered."

In another letter of about this time, seen for these notes only in partial transcript, [2] Crockett said that he was engaged in writing the history of his life and that Chilton was correcting this as he wrote it. In a letter to G. W. McLean, dated Washington City, January 17, 1834, Crockett again referred to the book: "As I consider no man on earth able to give a true history of my life I have undertaken this myself and will compleat it by the last of next week ready for

[1] In the Boston Public Library.
[2] In a Master's thesis by Margaret Gates, University of Illinois, 1929.

the press, and it will contain about two hundred pages." [1]

Chilton may have driven a hard bargain in the matter of profits, or Crockett—characteristically—may have been open-handed, but it seems clear that Crockett himself set down the substance of the "Narrative" on paper. Chilton may have written certain involved and heavy lines in the book on the political situation besides helping to "classify the matter." Some of the vocabulary has been considered above Crockett's command. It would be well not to dogmatize about Crockett's vocabulary. He had a natural sense of language and a growing aptitude in using it.

Only one other book of the time resembles the "Narrative" and this must be considered as partly Crockett's, though he resented its publication. This is

Sketches and Eccentricities of Col. David
Crockett of West Tennessee. New York, 1833.

The volume appeared anonymously. In the same year the same book was published in Cincinnati under the title, "The Life and Adventures of Colonel David Crockett of West Tennessee." The author's name is not given on the title page, but the copyright shows that of J. S. French, the reputed author of "Elkswatawa." In his "Chapter on Autography" Poe speaks of this biography of Crockett, written by French. The two volumes show a single variation. At the end of the "Sketches and Eccentricities" a note is added on the results of the election of 1833, favoring Crockett. At the end of the "Life and Adventures" appears a hunting sketch

[1] In the Library of Congress.

entitled "Billy Buck." It should perhaps be added that "Elkswatawa" has been ascribed to Timothy Flint in P. G. Thomson's "Catalogue of Books relating to Ohio."

For his "Narrative" Crockett helped himself to some of the stories in the "Sketches and Eccentricities," apparently copying these *verbatim*. The author had a genuine knack for setting them down, and Crockett, having told them, probably saw no reason why he should not take them back again as a short cut in the labor of writing. The "Sketches" contain certain materials not to be found elsewhere. These have been used in the present book whenever they have seemed consistent with known circumstances. Details from the "Sketches," as from the several books ascribed to Crockett, have frequently been transcribed here in the form in which they first appeared, because it could not be improved. The acknowledgment is made with candor and pleasure.

The "Narrative" must be ascribed to Crockett; and materials exist to indicate his share in the writing of the "Tour."

From Washington, on the 12th of January, 1835, Crockett wrote again to Carey and Hart, acknowledging the receipt of the title-page of a book which from the date can only be that of the "Tour." He had shown this to "Mr. Clark," he said, who had given him a package of manuscript which he was forwarding. "Am sorry there is not more of it done. I intend to try and have my part done this week or in the early part of next. Mr. Clark has been engaged in the Post Office Committee so that he cannot keep pace with me but he says he will soon be done and then he can in a few days finish." Crockett added, "You have stated that it is written by myself. I would rather if you think it could sell as well that you would have stated that it was written from notes furnished by myself." Finally he left the decision to the publishers.[1]

Now "Mr. Clark" may have been William Clark, member from Pennsylvania, who was for several years a member of the Public Expenditures Committee. But he was almost surely Matthew St. Clair Clarke, also of Pennsylvania, Clerk of the House, compiler of many volumes of congressional records, documents, and other archives, and Crockett's friend.[2] Clarke may have sat with the Post Office Committee. No Clark or Clarke appears as a member of that Committee. Derby[3] said that Matthew St. Clair Clarke collaborated with Crockett in the writing of the "Narrative." He may have meant the "Tour." Crockett's letter to Carey and Hart indicates the way in which the book was composed—from his own notes. The editing shows a neat, practiced hand, but the talk and the narrative are unmistakably Crockett's.

The crowd thickens of gentlemen associated with these books either in fact or by rumor. Mr. John A. Wade has argued[4] that the "Life of Martin Van Buren"—and indeed all of Crockett's books—were written by Augustine S. Clayton, a distinguished jurist of Georgia whom Crockett cer-

[1] In the collection of the New York Historical Society.
[2] "Diary of Christopher Baldwin." *Transactions and Collections of the American Antiquarian Society,* Vol. VIII.
[3] J. C. Derby, "Fifty Years Among Authors, Books, and Publishers." 1884.
[4] *Georgia Historical Quarterly,* 1922.

tainly knew. Many allusions to Georgia politics appear in the book, and it is possible that Clayton's son, who said that his father wrote a life of David Crockett, had in mind the "Life of Martin Van Buren." Hugh Lawson White of Tennessee has also been mentioned as the possible author of this skit. On the whole it is unimportant. Crockett may have had nothing to do with it; the book bears no traces of his characteristic style.

Still another contender for the authorship of a book ascribed to Crockett has been brought forward, Richard Penn Smith, the fluent author of many dramas, sketches, poems, a Philadelphian. The book in question is "Col. Crockett's Exploits and Adventures in Texas." Derby said that Smith wrote the book overnight, soon after word of Crockett's death was received in the East. This statement has been repeated by others, and seems to rest on an assertion in an article on Smith appearing in *Burton's Gentleman's Magazine* for September, 1839. This states that Smith wrote the book, "a work which has been the subject of much grave speculation." But if Smith wrote it, he would have been obliged to change his style overnight, indeed to adopt more than one style, for the early portion reads as though it had been rudely pieced together, while from the time the Texan adventure really begins it moves easily. And Smith never expressed on paper the kind of humor with which the "Exploits and Adventures" is filled.

Whoever wrote this book did not write it overnight, even with an arsenal of recent publications on Texas at his elbow. Such volumes were freely used; whole passages were taken over from Mrs. Holley's "Texas" and from David B. Edwards's "History of Texas," among others. But the outstanding figures of Thimblerig and the Bee Hunter can hardly have been chosen by accident, and the "Exploits" as a whole seems to have a partial basis in fact.

It is highly probable that Crockett wrote a number of letters on the journey to Texas. He would have abandoned a habit that was evidently agreeable to him if he had not done so. Almost surely he would have written to some of his friends, perhaps to political companions, in the East. The writer—or compiler—of the "Exploits and Adventures" may have had access to such letters. If they were written—to judge by Crockett's other correspondence—they would have contained many brief touches upon which a skillful writer could build. There is a further possibility. In the preface to the "Exploits and Adventures" mention is made of a diary of Crockett's, supposedly found on Castrillon's body at the battle of San Jacinto, who in turn was said to have taken it from Crockett's body at the Alamo. This statement has been ridiculed as fantastic, but it is not inherently so. The Mexican soldiers were permitted to rob the bodies at the Alamo; Crockett was recognized by Mexican officers. He would certainly have had papers. Letters or notes may have been among them. It is altogether possible that he was making notes for another book. Certainly in the summer of 1835 he was contemplating this. In a letter to Carey and Hart, dated July 8th, 1835, he said, "I have great hope of writing one more book." [1]

[1] From the catalogue of John Heise, Syracuse, New York.

BEHIND THIS BOOK

In "The Way to the West" Emerson Hough speaks of certain "correspondence" of Crockett's containing references to Jonathan Harrington Green, the great gambler of the day. Whether Thimblerig is a sketch of Green must remain an open question; Hough evidently believed that he was, but he does not cite his evidence. The correspondence to which Hough refers has not come to light, but a letter of Green's, dated June 5, 1884,[1] speaks of the voluminous notes on his life which he has kept for sixty-five years, mentions his knowledge of events in Texas during the Revolution, and refers to a connection with Crockett. Two of Green's books, "Gambling Unmasked" (1844) and "The Gambler's Life" (1857), though not mentioning Crockett, bear out the possibility of a meeting at this time by their descriptions of Green's movements.

Yet with all the possibilities of factual connection, "Col. Crockett's Exploits and Adventures" must be linked with the body of legend belonging to Crockett. He could hardly have enjoyed all the magnificent adventures attributed to him between its covers, even though any one of them is plausible. As to the writer—or compiler—some charming pieces of speculation may be indulged in, but they have no place here.

What again becomes plain is the careless wealth of Crockett's affiliations and the ease with legends clustered about his name. He was unique, surely, in being a man of stature with a significant career, and at the same time a character who even while living stepped straight into

[1] In the Yale University Library.

myth. And for lasting eminence he created a book, the "Narrative," that remains a classic in our literature because it was one of the first to use the American language with fullness and assurance, and because it reveals a way of life in a distinctive style.

A large collection of biographies and so-called autobiographies has developed out of the "Narrative," the "Tour," and the "Exploits and Adventures." With one exception these are abbreviations, redactions, or paraphrases, carelessly put together and containing many errors. In "The Autobiography of David Crockett, with an Introduction by Hamlin Garland" (New York, 1923) the three books are reprinted from the original editions; but the introduction repeats groundless assertions made in earlier biographies, particularly that of J. S. C. Abbott, and suffers from a straitened view as to Crockett's character.

The present book offers a certain body of material which hitherto has appeared only in Texas publications or in local tradition: this has to do with Crockett's journey into northeast Texas. The main account of the journey comes from Judge Pat V. Clark of Clarksville, Texas, whose grandmother followed Crockett on horseback from Clarksville and persuaded him to wait until a party could be formed to accompany him. This account is given in "Early Days in Red River County" by Claude V. Hall.[1] For the purposes of this book Mrs. T. M. Scott of Paris, Texas, has generously submitted further details gained from Judge Clark, with

[1] Bulletin of the East Texas State Teachers College, June, 1931.

evidence as to this journey gained from old settlers. Similar evidence has been considered through the kindness of Miss Elizabeth Downs of Temple, Texas, who has lent the writer letters written by descendants of settlers, recalling the definite tradition. The Dallas *Morning News* of January 6, 1894, carried an interview with Mrs. Clark, who vividly described her meeting with Crockett; a transcript of this interview has been seen because of sound research by Mr. Sam Acheson of this paper. The "lizard" or "spider," known as "Davy Crockett's spider," was kept in the Paris courthouse until the building burned in 1876, and is remembered by many old settlers.

The following books have been used to amplify or corroborate known facts as to Crockett's life in Tennessee:

Audubon, James. Ornithological Biography. Vols. I, II, III. Edinburgh, 1831-39.

—— The Quadrapeds of North America. New York, 1849-1854.

Davis, James D. History of the City of Memphis. Memphis, Tennessee, 1873.

Flint, Timothy. Recollections of the Last Ten Years. New York, 1932.

French, Mrs. J. Stewart, and Zella Armstrong. The Crockett Family and Connecting Lines. Bristol, Tennessee, 1928.

Guild, Joseph C. Old Times in Tennessee. Nashville, 1878.

Haywood, John. The Civil and Political History of Tennessee. Nashville, 1891.

Meine, Franklin J. Tall Tales of the Southwest. New York, 1930.

Mooney, James. Myths of the Cherokee. Report of the Bureau of Ethnology, 1897-99.

Moore, John Trotwood, and Austin P. Foster. Tennessee, the Volunteer State. Chicago, 1923.

Phelan, James. History of Tennessee. Boston, 1888.

Skinner, Constance Lindsay. Pioneers of the Old Southwest. New Haven, 1922.

[Williams, Joseph S.] Old Times in West Tennessee, by a Descendant of one of the First Settlers. Memphis, 1873.

Williams, Samuel Cole. Beginnings of West Tennessee in the Land of the Chickasaws, 1541-1841. Johnson City, Tennessee, 1930.

—— Early Travels in the Tennessee Country, 1540-1800. Johnson City, 1928.

For the Creek War and for Crockett's career in Congress the materials cited below have supplemented the "Register of Debates" and other works already mentioned:

Abel, Annie H. The History of Events Resulting in Indian Consolidation West of the Mississippi River. Annual Report of the American Historical Association, 1906.

Abernethy, T. P. From Frontier to Plantation in Tennessee. Chapel Hill, 1932.

Benton, Thomas H. Thirty Years' View. New York, 1861.

Foreman, Grant. Indian Removal. Norman, Oklahoma, 1932.

Parton, James. Life of Andrew Jackson. Boston, 1866.

Poore, Benjamin Perley. Reminiscences of

Sixty Years in the National Metropolis. Philadelphia, 1866.

Ross, John. To David Crockett, January 13, 1831. A. L. S. in the Newberry Library.

For the account of Crockett's journey through Arkansas and Louisiana the following books have been drawn upon:

Allsopp, Fred W. Folklore of Romantic Arkansas. Kansas City, 1931.

Dunn, Milton. History of Natchitoches. n. d. (pamphlet).

Herndon, Dallas. High Lights of Arkansas History, 1922.

Shinn, Josiah J. Pioneers and Makers of Arkansas. Little Rock, 1908.

Thorpe, Thomas B. The Mysteries of the Backwoods, 1846.

—— The Hive of the Bee Hunter, 1854.

Since Thorpe knew this region—and also western Tennessee—at approximately the time of Crockett's journey, and since his humor and tastes were akin to Crockett's, his sketches have been freely used.

The following works on Texas have yielded essential materials as to the final stages of Crockett's journey:

Bancroft, Hubert Howe. History of the North Mexican States and Texas. San Francisco, 1889.

Barker, Eugene C. Mexico and Texas, 1821-1835. Dallas, 1929.

Brown, John Henry. The History of Texas. 2 vols. St. Louis, 1893.

Castaneda, Carlos E. (editor). The Mexican Side of the Texas Revolution, 1836. Dallas, 1929.

Edwards, David B. History of Texas. Cincinnati, 1836.

Ford, John S. Origin and Fall of the Alamo. San Antonio, 1896.

Gray, A. C. From Virginia to Texas, 1835-1836. New York, 1909.

Holley, Mary Austin. Texas: Observations, Historical, Geographical and Descriptive. In a Series of Letters. Baltimore, 1833.

Kennedy, William. Texas: The Rise, Progress, and Prospects of the Republic of Texas. New York, 1841.

Lamar Papers, Vol. I-II. Austin, Texas, 1922.

Morphis, J. M. History of Texas. New York, 1874.

Smith, Justin. Annexation of Texas. New York, 1911.

Williams, Amelia. A Critical Study of the Siege of the Alamo and of the Personnel of its Defenders. A thesis presented to the Faculty of the Graduate School of the University of Texas in partial fulfilment of the requirements for the degree of Doctor of Philosophy. Austin, Texas, 1931.

Yoakum, H. History of Texas. New York, 1856.

Of the above, special mention must be made of Dr. Williams's "Study of the Siege of the Alamo and of the Personnel of its Defenders." This impressive work, lent by the

University of Texas Library in manuscript, has offered essential details drawn from documentary sources, and has provided an accurate check on research otherwise accomplished. It is impossible to list the many periodical articles used in the preparation of the present book.

For open-handed assistance of many kinds most cordial acknowledgments are offered to Mr. Clarence S. Brigham, Director of the American Antiquarian Society, Mr. Samuel H. Ranck, Librarian of the Grand Rapids Public Library, Mrs. John Trotwood Moore, Archivist and Librarian of the Tennessee State Library, Miss Libbie Morrow of Nashville, Miss Montgomery Cooper of Memphis, Mr. W. A. Provine, Librarian of the Tennessee Historical Society, Mr. Felix G. Woodward of Clarksville, Tennessee, Mr. Franklin J. Meine of Chicago, Miss Harriet Smither, Archivist of the Texas State Library, Mr. E. W. Winkler of the University of Texas Library, Mr. H. M. Lydenberg of the New York Public Library, Mr. M. A. Roberts, Superintendent of the Reading Room of the Library of Congress.

Mrs. J. Stewart French has generously permitted the use of a large collection of clippings, manuscripts, and other materials relating to Crockett and the Crockett family. Mrs. T. M. Hiner, Mrs. Seneca D. Powell, Judge W. A. Rhea, kindly have consented to the use of Crockett's letters in their possession. Miss Gladys Martin of Winchester, Tennessee, Mr. Edd Winfield Parks of Cumberland University, Dr. George Pullen Jackson of Vanderbilt University, Mr. Percy Mackaye, and Mr. Ben East of Grand Rapids have made valuable suggestions.

DAVY CROCKETT

Davy Crockett is the patron saint of the Dallas *News*. Its president, Mr. G. B. Dealey, has given momentum to the writing of this book; and Mr. Sam Acheson, one of its editors, has been a most friendly, patient collaborator. Mr. J. Frank Dobie, Miss Marcelle Hamer of Austin, and Mr. Robert K. Neill of San Angelo have offered assistance, as have Mrs. Joseph B. Nichols of Greenville, Texas, and Mrs. Cammie Garrett Henry of Melrose, Louisiana. Last and abundant thanks must go to the Reverend George L. Crocket of Nacogdoches, who has given materials out of his scholarly knowledge of Texas history and of the region in which he lives.